Terminal or Timeless

Betty B. Robison

CHAPTER ONE

Terminal or Timeless

*For I know the plans that I have for you, declares the Lord,
plans for welfare and not for calamity to give you a future
and hope.*

Jeremiah 29:11 (NIV)

They call it "Big Sky Country." It was almost dusk as we stood gazing at the ragged Beartooth Mountain Range to the north of us. From our perspective the range was dark and foreboding. I shivered a bit as I wrapped my sweater more tightly around me. We were safe and comfortable in the valley below. In a few hours most of us would be sleeping soundly in our comfortable R.V.'s.

Now, however, Robby was suggesting we hurry over to our friends, the Wiltons, for a game of dominoes. When we got there, Laura Wilton had prepared a blackberry cobbler and invited another couple from the camp to join us. We enjoyed the fellowship and fun of eating dessert together. As a matter of fact, we never did get around to playing dominoes. Laura asked her husband, Charley, to build a bonfire so we could sit outside and enjoy the stars. Heaven seemed so close in that cozy Montana setting. While we sat there discussing the day's activities we noticed a lone deer, a doe, walking into camp. She trod up and down several paths looking from side to side and, then, fled through the nearby meadow.

Laura commented that the wild animals seldom came down into the camp except in a dry season when they sought water. This was not the case now, so we were left wondering why the doe would come so close.

The next morning two of the camp staff told us that the day before they had seen a deer in the mountains above trying to fight off a brown bear. Apparently she had a newborn or very young offspring and the bear had killed it. He did what came naturally, hunted food when he was hungry and a young deer was easy prey. Even with the desperate mother trying to protect her child, in the animal kingdom she would have been no match for a brown bear. Fortunately, she herself managed to escape without being harmed.

As we stood discussing the bear's action someone offered, "That was probably the bereaved mother we saw in camp last evening."

I looked up to that mountain range and oddly enough there stood another doe. This one had just delivered a baby and was busy licking her offspring and nudging the infant to try standing on four wobbly legs. Finally the baby was up, nursing from its mother and getting stronger by the minute. In a matter of seconds the mother and child bounded into the brush out of our sight.

Later, over a cup of coffee, Laura and I were discussing what we had observed.

"You can't blame the bear for doing what bears do." Laura said.

I agreed but thought about it for a moment. "And wasn't God good to let us see another baby deer being born? All of this is part of a plan that is bigger than any of us. You know, we get so caught up in the individual incidents in our lives that we fail to realize that God is in control and has a much bigger plan than we know about."

Life does go on. Babies are born. Old people die. We live for the moment usually and expect everything to stay the same. Nothing does. I read one day, "Yesterdays pile on one another to make room for todays which too soon become tomorrows." I am reminded that if we live long enough we will grow old. It is inevitable and irreversible.

My husband, Robby, and I are growing old. Thank God together still. But sometimes we wonder, "How did we get here?" It seems only yesterday that we were young and vibrant and full of dreams. Most of our dreams now are either about the past or looking forward to heaven.

A friend, also named "Betty", has two sisters with Alzheimers disease. Betty's husband, Tom, told of how they had gone to these sisters' respective homes and taken the "girls" to a family gathering. As the younger family members rushed around preparing a large meal and children chased one another through the house, the sisters sat helplessly on the living room couch talking. Tom heard one sister ask the other, "How did we get here?" Both shook their heads. Neither knew or remembered that Tom and Betty had picked them up at home. It was both sad and amusing to Tom.

The Bible indicates that there will be no need for time keeping in Heaven. We might as well throw away our watches. God has a schedule that transcends time. I wonder if that is why small children often seem to have no comprehension of time? Today as I walked our dog, four year old neighbor, Liam, ran out of his house to show me his toy car. He asked to pet Misty, the dog, and then jumped from one large rock in their yard to another. He was very proud of his accomplishments. All this time his mother, Rebecca, was trying desperately to get Liam into the house to eat cereal before she took him to pre-school.

Liam lives entirely in the present. One hour from now might as well not exist. Liam's outlook seems so simple and so right in our hectic hurry, hurry world. Yet, much as we might want to, none of us can live that way. God established time to regulate our lives on this earth. Our clocks and watches control us and keep life orderly. Usually our lives are orderly. When I stop to think about it, though, I believe I am going to like living in an eternity where time doesn't matter. The Bible also teaches us that with God "a day is as a thousand years", or vice versa.

Several years ago I had developed a chronic dry cough. It became so constant that I went to the doctor to check it out. He explored several possibilities, including possible allergies. Then he asked, "Do you smoke or have you ever smoked?"

I hadn't, but his next question hit the nail on the head. "Were you ever exposed to second hand smoke for long periods of time?"

My answer, of course, was "Yes, when I was a legal secretary in Kansas." My boss was a chain smoker and most of the other attorneys smoked also. I sat in smoke filled rooms for hours taking dictation. Our offices probably were never free of smoke, even in the small room I had been assigned. Some attorney was always coming into or passing through my office. I didn't even know smoking, let alone second hand smoke, was dangerous to one's health. I know better now and, years later was sorry to hear that my first attorney boss had developed lung cancer and shot himself rather than suffer.

When I explained those early years to my doctor he nodded, "Well, I am certain you have chronic bronchitis." I thought *Oh well, an occasional case of bronchitis isn't so bad.* Then the doctor gave me more information about the ailment. It is a matter of the bronchi being damaged. They cannot be repaired and there is no cure for chronic bronchitis.

The next evening our son, Denny, called to check on his "elderly" parents. I told him about the doctor's prognosis and then moaned, "Denny, I'm terminal."

Denny, ever logical, replied, "Mom, we're all terminal." Of course, it's just a matter of time. But we are so used to living in the here and now that we do not think much about dying. That's somewhere in the distant future. I'll think about it tomorrow.

Tomorrow is here and, like it or not, I really must think about it now.

Our pastor stated the other Sunday, "Fifty years from now most of us won't be here. Certainly, not one hundred years from now."

Robby's and my ailments are physical but real. I was digging through a box of pictures the other day as I looked for a particular baby picture of granddaughter, Tina. I came upon two photographs of us taken many years ago when our boys were small. Even before the girls were born. We looked so young. There were no visible wrinkles and both had dark hair. *I must show these to Rob.*

My husband took one look at the old photos and commented, "Those were taken a hundred years ago." Well, not quite. True, the time between then and now was lengthy but it seems like only yesterday those pictures were made. We are certainly not the same people we were then. I hope we have grown spiritually and emotionally, but in many ways I feel like the same person.

Rob couldn't help asking, "How did we get here?"

CHAPTER TWO

Hope for Tomorrow

*When a wicked man dies, his expectation will perish, and
the hope of strong men perishes. Proverbs 11:7 (NAS)
And whosoever liveth and believeth in me shall never die.
Believest thou this?*

John 11:26 (KJV)

With four children at home, both Robby and I working,
our lives were busy. Every Saturday I did loads of
laundry, a little ironing and straightening and cleaning the
house. I made up hundreds of sandwiches to freeze. We'd
add the lettuce and condiments later. Fortunately the children
didn't like the school cafeteria lunches much. We couldn't
afford to buy them anyway.

During the week it seemed we were always rushing
somewhere. Neither Rob nor I had time to consider that this
way of life would not last. What seemed an eternity was
really only a short time. As I said before, God has a different
time schedule than most of us.

Now, flash forward thirty years—our nest is empty.
We await the telephone calls on weekends to keep up with
the activities of children and grandchildren. The greatest

excitement today is news of birth of our second great grandson. We received the call telling us they named him Tyler. I liked that but wondered how we could ever find a nickname (like Tommy or Billy). I suspect the parents would prefer he not have a nickname. I still insist on calling our youngest "Jennifer" when everyone else calls her "Jenny".

Daily we face our mortality. God comforts us on every hand. Those Bible promises we've collected for years are more meaningful than ever. I confess we get a bit fearful when something life threatening happens.

I recall how a few years ago when a nerve tumor in my throat began to grow. It was located between the carotid artery and the jugular vein. Not easy for the surgeon to remove. I was later told about the number of nerve trunks in that area. Severing any one of them could have left my face permanently impaired. For some reason, I was not fearful at the time. A friend asked me if I were and I replied, "No, I know that when the operation is over and I awake I will either be looking in the face of Robby or Jesus. Either one would be wonderful." Rob told someone later when recounting that conversation of mine, "I think she was disappointed when she saw it was me."

Of course I wasn't disappointed. But neither had I been worried about the other possibility.

So many people were praying before and during the surgery that it was mind boggling. I called a Bible Study Fellowship friend in Southern California and she assured me the entire class and others would be praying.

I received a telephone call one evening from a friend in Paradise, California, whom I had met in church. She said, "I wanted to know if you would mind if I turned your name in to a prayer group I belong to? We pray literally around the world. Our members actually circle the globe." How could I object to that?

Everyone I talked with had a Bible verse or promise to share. On the day before we were to leave our home and drive the hundred miles to Sacramento to the Kaiser hospital two of our church's pastors came to visit and pray with me. Naturally, they had reassuring Scripture to share with me. After the pastors had left I felt a little bewildered. Why had I not claimed one of the many suggested passages of Scripture for my own? I sat down to read my Bible and opened it to the book of Psalms. I read Psalm 94:19. *In the multitude of my thoughts within me thy comforts delight my soul. (KJV)* God was reminding me that over the years I had claimed many passages of Scripture for my own. He certainly spoke to me that day and I felt as though He were saying *"Be still and know that I am God."* He was truly all I needed.

Some days in this stage of my life on earth I just need to go back to those promises and remember who God is. He knows I'm old, as man measures "old" but with God time is not an issue. In Heaven we'll be forever young. God's plan is perfect and He can be trusted to carry out every part of His plan for my life, here and on into the endless ages of eternity.

Another precious memory has to do with Robby. Claudia was just a baby when he had an operation for appendicitis. He recovered nicely from the surgery and was soon back at work. A short time after that, however, he became ill with an undefined infection. The doctors were puzzled and considered sending him to the UCLA Medical Center for more tests or treatments.

I was frightened. The doctor suspected some rare blood disease. I knew I could lose my husband. I felt ill-equipped at the time to become a single mom to two small boys and a baby girl.

One day in my desperation I bundled up the baby and drove to Inglewood to my folks' house. The boys were in school and Robby had gone to work. I knew he should have stayed home that day but he was concerned because his hourly pay was too low for us to save any money. Sick pay was not a part of our lives at that time.

When I got to Inglewood, both parents welcomed the baby and took turns holding her. I began to cry and explained how worried I was about Robby. I sobbed, "Would you pray with me?" I had been praying on my own for several weeks but, for some reason, did not feel my prayers were getting past the ceiling.

I put Claudia on the floor on a blanket and handed her a chewing toy. She was cutting teeth and loved to chew on most anything. She was a good baby and easily entertained so I felt comfortable kneeling at the sofa there beside her. Mother and Daddy knelt beside their chairs.

First, I poured out my heart to the Lord, explaining how I couldn't raise the children alone. I asked specifically that God would heal Robby, and soon. My Mother prayed a similar prayer and then Daddy prayed.

He began by praising the Lord for giving them children and grandchildren. *Get to the point, Daddy.* Then my father thanked God for being all knowing and all powerful. He did ask that God would touch my husband with His healing hand. He closed with, "We know that you know best and we trust you to do your will. Our desire is that your will be done in this matter."

After the final "Amen," I got Claudia back in the car to leave. I was in a hurry to get out of there. Daddy's words weren't what I had wanted to hear. I thought on the way home, *What if it is God's will to take my precious husband now and leave me with all that responsibility?* I did not want that. I was almost angry with my father for his prayer.

All the way home I argued with the Lord. I was hanging on to what I wanted with all the will power I had. The struggle went on for several miles. Finally, just before driving in our driveway I let go. With tears rolling down my face I submitted. I let go and my prayer changed. *It's all right, Father. You have been so real to me in the past. I know that whatever you have planned for me is best. Help me now not to hold on to the things I want, even if it is my wonderful husband. He's yours and I can trust you to do what is best for us. Thank you.*

That evening Robby was much better. He recovered without our knowing what the ailment was. It was serious, of course, but totally in God's hands. I learned a lesson on letting go and letting God take over.

Now, in this latter part of my life on this earth as I know it, I need God's reassurance more than ever. I've developed a helpful habit in fearful, frightening times. I say, "Jesus, please hold my hand." It's almost like I've become a child again. Jesus is always there. I don't know how it works but it does.

Our precious Jennifer, youngest of the four, suffers from Parkinson's Disease. I shared with her my secret of getting calm. She said she tried it, too, and it helped. She has claustrophobia and needs the Savior's touch when undergoing an MRI or myriads of other treatments or tests.

I know that asking Jesus to hold my hand is more than a mere ritual or magic formula. It is an act of faith. Sometimes we need to act out our faith in tangible ways.

When grandson, Christopher, was a little boy he sang lustily most every song he heard. One day when we were babysitting him I looked out the window and saw that little guy standing on the curb singing at the top of his lungs, "**Put your hand in the hand of the man from Galilee.**" I doubt he really knew what it meant but he was certainly enjoying singing about it. I enjoyed his performance and hoped the neighbors did also.

I wish I were as bold as Chris was that day when I attempt to tell others about Jesus. There are so many frightened folks in the world today who don't know that God has provided Hope for Tomorrow for every fearful one of us.

CHAPTER THREE

Fear and Trembling

After this, the word of the Lord came to Abram in a vision:
"Do not be afraid, Abram
I am your shield,
your very great reward."

Genesis 15:1 (NIV)

Late one afternoon I received a call from my friend, Nancy. In a very calm voice she said, "Betty, I cannot reach the Prayer Chain. Will you call them for me? I came home awhile ago and found Lee slumped over his computer. His eyes were open but fixed."

I interrupted her, "Nancy, is anyone with you?"

She answered, still strangely calm. "No, but I am driving to the hospital right now. The ambulance took Lee."

My "do something" mode went into effect. "Robby and I will drive to the hospital at once." Rob was taking a late nap and I hurried in to wake him. Then I called the head of the Prayer Chain and gave her the news and prayer request.

Robby and I rushed around to get our shoes on, feed the dog and jump in the car for the twenty minute drive to the hospital. When we arrived and asked at the front desk where

Nancy was, a friendly volunteer escorted us back to the "family room." The hospital has furnished some small rooms for such emergencies. Our Sunday School teacher, Larry and his wife, Willie, were there with Nancy. Also present was a volunteer, a lovely lady who introduced herself as a member of the "trauma team." She served as a liaison between all of us and Lee. She offered to get us coffee or juice and then she checked to make sure the ER team was ready for Nancy to go in to see Lee.

Meantime, a Paramedic had come by to tell Nancy he had been in the ambulance with Lee and that Lee was still breathing. We didn't know then but Lee was not breathing on his own but with the help of the life support system.

Scans and tests showed that Lee had suffered a brain aneurysm. It was decided that he would be flown to Phoenix to a large hospital where a brain surgeon was available to operate. It was agreed that Larry and Willie would drive Nancy in her car to Phoenix and Robby and I would follow to bring our friends back to Prescott. All of us were still hopeful that surgery would save Lee's life.

Nancy had her cell phone with her and called their sons and daughter in New York. The three children arrived the next day and, after much prayer and deliberation, it was decided to disconnect the life support system. We think Lee had already died.

Both Robby and I were shaken at the sudden loss of a friend we had known for some time. Next, we both began to think that it really could have been either of us. At our age and in the condition of our health we know we must face the fact that our time on this earth as we know it is short.

A few days after that we received word that a favorite niece, Cindi, had lost her husband, Ted. Ted had not yet retired from work and both of them were hoping to buy a home in Arizona later.

I admit to having a fearful heart when I think of living without my husband. He seems to be very calm but frustrated that he can no longer be as active as he once was. We had anticipated driving to California to have Christmas with all our children and to see our latest great grandson for the first time. However, when Robby had a treadmill test he did not do well and the Cardiologist ordered an angiogram to determine what was wrong. He said he felt there was a blockage in one of the cardiac arteries. Naturally, we cancelled our trip and decided to spend Christmas at home in Arizona.

On a routine visit to my primary care doctor I noted all my aches and pains but commented, "I guess at age 84 it is not unusual to have these symptoms." Dr. Gale became thoughtful, "Well, if life is a continuum, age is not important—64, 84 or 94. All ages should be at their best to do what has to be done."

When I got home, I looked up the word, continuum in Webster's Dictionary. It said, "continuum, n. a continuous extent, series, or whole, with no discernible division into parts." Hmm, *life is a series of segments. Our time on this earth as we know it, is a very small part of the whole.*

Now, I thought, look up mortality. Webster said, "mortality, the state or condition of being subject to death."

All of this really set me thinking. I *am* fearful often. I just don't like the idea of facing the unknown. I try to understand how it would be to live in another dimension. Any other dimension than the one I am living in is a total unknown. Little did I know that I would soon be faced with unknown and frightening circumstances which might try my faith.

CHAPTER FOUR

Family Ties

*For you have not received a spirit of slavery leading to fear
again, but you have received a spirit of adoption as sons by
which we cry out, "Abba! Father!"*

Romans 8:15 (NAS)

We had just finished dinner and I set about cleaning up
the kitchen and preparing the coffee to go on automatically the next morning. Robby complained that he was
having a bit of indigestion and should lie down for a few
minutes. When I had finished in the kitchen I went into the
bedroom. Rob said he was actually having heavy pressure in
his chest. I sat with him for a few minutes and knew he obviously was extremely uncomfortable. He does not often share
his aches and pains as I do. Finally, he said, "I think you had
better call 911." *This must be serious. Do it now.* I called 911
and explained what was happening. They promised to be at
the house within a few minutes.

I next called my brother, Richard and his wife Merna,
and asked if they would come over and go with me to the
hospital. They were at our door right after the paramedics
arrived. How thankful I was that my younger sibling and his

wife had not left for California as they intended to do the next week.

Rob was transported to the hospital by ambulance while Richard, Merna and I followed in Richard's car.

After the E.R. doctors had Rob stabilized it was decided to admit him to the hospital so that he could have an angiogram the next day. It had originally been scheduled for a week later. The next day Richard and Merna accompanied me to await the angiogram. When the Cardiologist came out he announced that the suspected blockage proved to be 99 per cent. Frightening. He added that he felt they could take care of it with a stent.

That was reassuring. Placing a stent in the artery is a common procedure. As a matter of fact, I have one in a major cardiac artery and know that in most cases the hospital stay is just overnight. When I told our children about the procedure, Claudia immediately began to arrange for someone to be with me. Robby was required to stay in our local hospital for the week between Christmas and New Years in order to go down to St. Joseph's Hospital in Phoenix when more of the surgeons would be on duty.

Our oldest son, Denny, came from California to accompany me to Phoenix and to be there for the angioplasty. Our children must have done considerable telephoning and rearranging their lives to be with us when we needed them.

In Phoenix, at St. Joseph's Hospital, the resident Cardiologist met us with disturbing news. He felt certain that from all the pictures, open heart surgery was the safest procedure. Denny had a five-way coronary by-pass several years before. He is doing well and reassured me that it was wise to follow the doctor's advice even though it would mean a longer hospital stay and recovery period at home. After much prayer and a desire to trust completely in God's provision, Robby and I agreed to proceed with the surgery.

Denny and I settled in for several hours' wait until the surgery was finished. We were both praying quietly. When the surgeon finally came out he announced that Robby had come through the surgery well. We could see our husband and father as soon as the nurses had him cleaned up and settled in the recovery room. Denny and I breathed a sigh of relief. *So glad it's finally over.* As we sat waiting for the nurse to come for us, I prayed *Thank you, Lord, for caring for Robby. He's yours and I know he could never be in better hands. Thank you! Thank you!*

A nurse came rushing in and sat down beside us. She said, "I'm sorry, but we are sending Mr. Robison back into surgery. There is extreme bleeding. We need to open him up again. I'll be back soon to give an update."

Why is this happening, Father? You've provided so much help this far. Why?

Denny called Claudia on his cell phone to ask her to be praying. After talking to her for a few minutes, he handed me the phone.

"She wants to talk to you, Mom."

Claudia knew I was struggling. "Hi, Mom. How are you doing?" I broke. "Not well at all." Claudia promised her family would pray. I sobbed, "Thanks. Goodbye."

I really began to cry and Denny hugged me. *Children are one of God's greatest blessings. Thank you, Lord.*

I knew I was having an emotional repeat of my experience when Claudia was a baby. I was hanging on tightly to something (or someone) I loved. I was not trusting my Heavenly Father to do what was best for us. *After all, hadn't he already protected and spared Robby's life?* I took that as a sign He was not going to require our separation at this time. It might also have meant that I had chosen to cling to my own desires.

Once I realized what was happening, I mentally chose to open both hands and pray *Everything I have, Oh Lord, is yours. I choose now to trust.* Letting go is hard. We are such self-involved creatures, but God will help us even to let go. We just need to be willing. A dear friend and teacher once said "I pray and ask God to help me be willing to be willing. He always answers my prayer. That is when He can begin to manifest His great power and great love."

I don't think we fully realize how much God loves us. Oh, I know most of us brought up in Christian homes early on memorized John 3:16. (*For God so loved the world that He gave His only begotten son, that whosoever believeth in him should not perish but have everlasting life.*) That verse, learned by rote when we were children, when lived out later, guarantees our entry into Heaven. We choose to believe that Jesus is the way and we will escape an eternity in Hell if we accept what Jesus Christ did for us on the cross. All of this is true, of course, but it doesn't even begin to explain the depth of God's love for His children.

Claudia told me later what was happening at her house after she talked with me on the phone. Two of our grandchildren, Becky and Will, were home. As Claudia hung up the phone, she motioned to those children.

"Come sit beside me and pray for Grandpa."

They sat down and bowed their heads. Claudia was shaken and emotions were too near the surface to speak. She said the three of them sat silently for fifteen minutes. Everyone was praying, of course.

Grandchildren are also God's gift to us. Thank you, Lord.

As for Denny and me, after what seemed a very long time, the nurse came back out. She reported, "We still have not found the source of the bleeding. The doctor does not want to close him up until he finds it."

Finally, I was calm. God's love and power were working in me. More waiting and trusting. At last, the doctor came out in his scrubs. His first words were, "He's fine. We have sewed him back up and have the bleeding under control. He doesn't even know what he's been through and will be out until tomorrow morning. You may as well get some sleep now."

Thank you, Lord, for good doctors.

As Denny and I walked down the hall he put his arm around me and said,

"Mom, you know God has spared Dad for awhile longer. But you may have to face losing him in the future. Or he will have to face losing you."

I wondered how this oldest son can be so wise. Perhaps it is because the first two years of his life he was "the man of the house." Of course he didn't know what that meant but I did.

Early in our marriage I had to face the possibility of losing my husband in World War II. Robby was drafted into the Navy Seabees a few weeks before Denny was born. He wasn't discharged until Denny was two and a half.

When Robby was in the Navy Seabees he was stationed in Hawaii as a stevedore loading and unloading ships. From time to time different battalions were moved out to some of the islands to prepare landing strips for the Marines. These were always very dangerous places to be.

One night I began to feel really worried about my husband. I sat up half the night praying for his safety. About two o'clock in the morning I began to have a strong sense of peace. It seemed that God was saying to my heart, "Go to bed. He is safe."

Years later Rob shared with me that the night I was concerned, his battalion had, indeed, been ready to ship out to one of the more dangerous islands. He said they waited for several hours until, finally, they received orders to stay where they were. Another battalion had been sent instead. I remember when he gave me this account he rather ruefully said, "I was kind of disappointed. How am I going to tell my grandchildren how their grandfather fought in the war but stayed all that time in Hawaii?" I assured him that he was my hero and would surely be the same to his grandchildren. I was thankful God had intervened.

Yes, I know that because I am eighty-four years of age and Robby is eighty-two we need to consider being separated. The most important lesson God has taught me over the years is that I cannot hold tightly to anything or anyone. God is totally in control.

Some time ago, I began thinking about death. If I am going to spend eternity with God, shouldn't I know Him better? There are so many things I don't know. I want to know how to worship in a pleasing way. I want to feel God's presence.

There are so many questions. What will we be doing for all eternity? The Bible says there is no marriage in Heaven. We believers will be the Bride of Christ. In addition the Bible says we are part of the family of God when we have made Christ our personal Savior. That would make Robby and me, and our children and so many more all part of one larger family than we can ever experience here on this earth today. And, yet I am a bit fearful.

The family ties we have on earth provide such comfort, joy and stability. I don't like the thought of giving that up but I love to contemplate what eternity will be like. Almighty God who originally established the family has promised to provide a family atmosphere beyond anything we can imagine. Why should I be fearful? I should, instead, be joyfully expectant. And thanking God everyday that we are at this time in our lives, right on the verge of the next segment of God's great plan for us. Family ties in glory!

CHAPTER FIVE

Meantime – Here and Now

I urge you therefore, brethren, by the mercies of God, to present your bodies a living and holy sacrifice, acceptable to God, which is your spiritual service of worship.

Romans 12:1

Dr. Francis Schaeffer wrote a book entitled *How Should We Then Live?* We need, at this time in our lives, to ask the same question. We know God has great plans for our future. Life as we know it now is often full of sorrow, pain, disappointment and frustrations. All of that, apparently, will disappear in eternity with Christ. So here we are and, in the meantime, how should we live?

We received a wonderful e-mail with the subject "And Then It Is Winter." Winter is referring to this time in our lives. Under a picture of a loving "older" couple are these words:

You know, time has a way of moving quickly and catching you unaware of the passing years.

It seems just yesterday that I was a young girl, just married and embarking on my new life with my husband.

And yet in a way, it seems like eons ago, and I wonder where all the years went. I know that I lived them all... And I have glimpses of how it was back then and of all my hopes and dreams...

But here it is...the winter of my life and it catches me by surprise...How did I get here so fast? Where did the years go and where did my babies go? And where did my youth go?

I remember well...seeing older people through the years and thinking that those older people were years away from me and that winter was so far off that I could not fathom it or imagine fully what it would be like...

But here it is...husband retired and he's really getting gray...he moves slower and I see an older man now. He's in better shape than me...but, I see the great change...

Not the one I married who was dark and young and strong..but, like me, his age is beginning to show and we are now those older folks that we used to see and never thought we'd be.

Each day now, I find that just getting a shower is a real target for the day! And taking a nap is not a treat anymore...it's mandatory! Cause if I don't on my own free will...I just fall asleep where I sit!

And so, now I enter into this new season of my life unprepared for all the aches and pains and the loss of strength and ability to go and do things.

But, at least I know, that though the winter has come, and I'm not sure how long it will last... This I know, that when it's over...I will enjoy the Spring in the arms of my loving Father... and wait for my loved ones to come when their winter is over too.

There was more to that e-mail which really encouraged younger folks to do what they needed to do now before it is too late. I very much enjoyed the first part, however, because it expresses what I am feeling. Where did the time go? Also, I need to be thinking seriously about what I should be doing in the meantime before God takes me into that eternal Springtime.

Now that Robby is recovering from his heart surgery we feel more certain than ever that God has left us here for a reason. We may never know all the reasons—God knows. We are sure, though, that it is our responsibility to seek God's will and His purpose. The Bible gives many guidelines and directions which we have been learning over the years. One very foundational truth for all believers is that the Holy Spirit is constantly causing us to be more like Christ. That process is being brought about by God's Holy Spirit before we go to live in God's eternal presence.

Which brings me to another conclusion. God's word states that we are to be holy as God is holy. How in the world can miserable little me be holy like God? Only through the miraculous work of the Holy Spirit I'm sure. I intend to try to focus on that aspect of my character this week. I have discovered that finding the appropriate Bible verses and meditating on them helps accomplish my goal. So.....

Romans 12:1 – I beseech you therefore, brethren, by the mercies of God, that ye present your bodies as a living sacrifice, <u>holy,</u> acceptable unto God, which is your reasonable service. *Well, that is certainly a basic command. It doesn't say you have to be young and vibrant or even particularly talented. Just be available for whatever God asks you to do.*

I Corinthians 3:16-17 – Know ye not that ye are the temple of God, and that the Spirit of God dwelleth in you? If any man defile the temple of God, him shall God destroy; for the temple of God is <u>holy,</u> which temple ye are. *So maybe the command here is that I take better care of this old body of mine as long as I have it.*

I Peter 1:14-16 – As obedient children, not fashioning yourselves according to the former lusts in your ignorance: but as he which hath called you is <u>holy,</u> so be ye <u>holy</u> in all manner of conversation; because it is written, be ye <u>holy;</u> for I am <u>holy.</u> *Somehow, I get the impression that God is commanding me to be holy, not just try to be. So it must be possible for me to live a holy life. I think that requires keeping very short accounts. When I sin and the Holy Spirit points it out to me I need to do exactly as I John 1:9 says: "If we confess our sins, He is faithful and righteous to forgive us our sins and to cleanse us from all unrighteousness." When I fall off the holiness wagon I need to confess it at once and get right back on. Help me, Father, to be obedient to your commands.*

In speaking of holiness, Peter says in I Peter 2:1: "Laying aside all malice, and all guile, and hypocrisies, and envies, and all evil speakings," *Now that is quite a list of things I need to be "laying aside" or, in other words, "getting rid of" in my daily life.*

"Malice" – I don't really have a problem there. The dictionary says that word means: "a desire to inflict harm or suffering on another." No, I don't do that. On to the next word. "Guile" – "insidious cunning in attaining a goal; crafty or artful deception, deceit." I could brush that aside

as something I don't do but I believe I need to think about it further.

"Hypocrasies" – "the false profession of desirable or publicly approved qualities, beliefs or feelings, especially a pretense of having virtues, moral principals or religious beliefs that one does not really possess." Well, well, how often have I mentioned some instance of a successfully taught Bible lesson or good deed for a friend? I think our hearts deceive us often. Being a hypocrite is probably the greatest deterrent to living a holy life. My prayer would be "Dear Father, help me to be totally transparent as a Christian. Help me not to build up myself but build up others every day."

"Envies" – I know I sometimes envy others who are more affluent, more influential as writers, speakers or just people. Webster describes the word envy as "begrudging admiration." Oops! I'd better watch out for that.

"Evil speakings" – I think that means saying bad things about others. I don't knowingly do that. However, I have repeated some bad things I've heard or know to be true about others. "Forgive me, Father, for repeating bad reports."

2 Peter 3:11. Seeing then that all these things shall be dissolved, what manner of persons ought ye to be in all holy conversation and godliness. *I've always been one to speak too quickly and sometimes too much. I must consider what "holy conversation" means if I plan to live a holy life. Perhaps my daily prayer could be, "Please, Father, will you guide my tongue today? Help me to be more sensitive to the prodding or nudging of your Holy Spirit."*

Romans 6:22. "But now being made free from sin, and become servants to God, ye have your fruit unto holiness and the end everlasting life." *So I am in a position to become holy because of what Christ has done for me. And the beauty of it is that I shall live forever in that position. "Thank you, Lord."*

As I mentioned before, it is God's will that each of His children be conformed to Christ, or as I see it, "to be more like Christ." In Galatians 5:22 and 23 we have the "fruit of the Spirit" listed. "Love, joy, peace, patience, kindness, goodness, faithfulness, gentleness, self-control." Some translations say "a sound mind" instead of "self-control." I can see how they are similar.

Last week I focused on becoming "holy." That is one of God's commands, that as His child I become holy as He is holy. As I examined many aspects of holiness I found myself falling far short of what God may want me to be. However, the exercise was helpful because I was aware of the Holy Spirit prodding me at times. It was almost like someone saying, "Is that a pure motive?" No, back off. Ask God's forgiveness and start over. It is so easy to kid ourselves but God sees through our intentions. He is so faithful to keep us on the right track if we cooperate.

Now, this week I'd like to focus on "joy." I remember years ago when one of my young leaders in the Bible study I was teaching confessed she felt no joy in her salvation.

We prayed about it and I looked up a page of Bible verses on joy from the Naves Topical Bible. I asked her to prayerfully review each of those verses and I was sure God would strengthen and comfort her through them. I believe it worked because she soon became a cheerful and fun person to be with.

Sometimes I don't feel joyful. I feel old and weak and vulnerable. It helps just to quote "The joy of the Lord is my strength." (Nehemiah 8:10b) Following are a few of the verses I find helpful:

Psalm 16:11 "Thou wilt shew me the path of life: in thy presence is fullness of joy; at thy right hand there are pleasures for evermore." *Now there's a promise from God, Himself. He has promised to show me the way to live. The only condition for being joyful in it is that I be in His pres-*

ence. One thing I know—I don't pray enough. Could it be that reading more of His word and spending more actual time in prayer is needed? I'm afraid I know the answer. Perhaps I might concentrate on being a more disciplined person. Eccl. 2:26. "For God giveth to a man that is good in His sight wisdom, and knowledge, and joy: but to the sinner He giveth travail, to gather and to heap up, that He may give to him that is good before God. *I am so grateful that God promises me wisdom, knowledge and joy. It seems that I must seek His will and His approval every day of my life if I am to be considered "good in His sight." Please keep me there, Father.*

Isaiah 12:3. "Therefore with joy shall ye draw water out of the wells of salvation." *I know I am saved through the blood of Jesus Christ who died for me. So I am promised joy. Thank you, Lord.*

Galatians 5:22. "The fruit of the Spirit is love, joy, peace,...." We read the rest of that verse before. I think today I'd like to focus my attention on God's great love for me. It is more than I can comprehend. The more I think about God's love for me the more I tend to love others. Last week my sister, Charlotte, died. I'm the oldest in this family of ten children and, according to some, should be the first to leave this earth. God has other plans apparently. I feel very sad, of course. When we were children, Charlotte was the sassy fun-loving sister. She played little jokes on the more serious, practical Dorothy, argued incessantly with me and generally was the center of everyone's attention much of the time. She has not been physically well for many years and I am sorry she has had so much suffering. Even her mind seemed to deteriorate over the years as she was subjected to so many different pain medications. Now I know she has a clear mind and strong body as she is in that eternal Springtime of Jesus' presence. I actually look forward to visiting with her and sharing some of those precious moments of eternity when my Springtime begins. Meantime, I'm shedding a few tears here and now. Just can't help it.

CHAPTER SIX

God's Great Love

For God so loved the world, that he gave his only begotten Son, that whosoever believeth in him should not perish, but have everlasting life.

John 3:16 (KJV)

God's love is beyond my comprehension. I can't imagine willingly giving up either of my sons. They are so precious and have contributed so much to my happiness over the years that I tend to hang on tightly. Yet I know that they belong to the Heavenly Father and He has a plan for their lives. It could be entirely different from any plan I may have had. I suppose the question is: "Do you love God enough to let Him have His way with all your loved ones?" *Father, that is my prayer today. Please help me to surrender every thing in life to you.*

Romans 8:28 "And we know that all things work together for good to them that love God. *Please, Father add to the above prayer another: Help me to love you as I should. I know then that all things will work out for good.*

Deuteronomy 6:5. "And thou shalt love the Lord thy God with all thine heart, and with all thy soul, and with all thy

might." *That sounds as though God is really serious about my attitude toward Him. Please Dear Father remind me each day not to be half hearted in my devotion and service to you.*
I John 4:19. "We love him, because he first loved us." *The reason is plain. God loved us and we love Him back.*
I John 4:7. Let us love one another: for love is of God; and every one that loveth is born of God, and knoweth God. *It seems that God Himself supplies the love. I can't dredge it up, add to it or take it away. It is there if we belong to Him. Thank you, Jesus.*

The dictionary does not do the word "love" justice. Especially as it relates to my relationship to God. One of the many explanations reads: "the benevolent affection of God for His creatures, or the reverent affection due from them to God." The remainder of the explanations have to do with "sex." Sex today has become a sideline of almost everything except genuine love.

The love I have for God and His Son, Jesus Christ, always spills over into my relationship with others. When I am feeling especially close to Christ I find it easy to love those around me.

I believe it helps to recall the many instances in the past when someone has treated me kindly and lovingly. All of those times have helped shape me into the person I am today.

Growing up, the oldest of ten children, during the Great Depression our family was very poor. Christmas usually meant that many of our wishes went unfulfilled. Mother and Daddy tried to get a little candy and fruit to put in our stockings. Large presents were almost unheard of. In my book, *Tomorrow's Troubles,* I have written about an incident of love portrayed by my mother.

"I went to sleep at once that Christmas Eve. I was aroused by the sound of the sewing machine. *It must be almost morning.* Puzzled, I slipped quietly out of bed and tiptoed toward the dining room where she sewed. Her back was to me and she didn't see me standing in the doorway. She finished a long seam and held up the garment to inspect it. I could see it was an outing flannel nightgown just the right length for me. I sensed it was best not to be discovered and tiptoed back to my bedroom. I slid noiselessly into bed and lay awake for awhile thinking of the love I had just seen displayed. My mother, tired as I knew she had to be, staying up after everyone had gone to bed in order to have her gift for me finished, wrapped and under the tree on Christmas morning. It was more than just a new night-gown, which I truly needed. Mother was giving a part of herself. I glimpsed a little of the true meaning of Christmas. Could I ever love so well?"

I remember, years later, lying in a hospital bed in Manhattan, Kansas, awaiting the arrival of our first child. Robby was in Idaho in Navy Boot Camp. Both his mother and mine were taking excellent care of me as was the hospital staff. All I could think about was how much I missed my husband and wishing he were present for this most important event. I had spent one night in difficult labor and was becoming very tired and frustrated. At one point Mother said to me, "Well, honey, don't you want ten babies?" Even if she'd had ten babies at home I didn't want to think about it. In my angry, resentful state of mind, I decided her remark was a little inconsiderate anyway.

In the morning a little nun came rushing in and introduced herself as the hospital's bookkeeper. She said, "My dear, I'm afraid we are going to have to move you into a ward. The government will not pay for this private room." I began to cry. "I don't care. We have some money saved. I'll pay the difference." I can't recall now why it seemed so important to me. I had volunteered in this hospital as a Red Cross Nurse's Aid when we first moved from Wichita to Manhattan. After working for many hours I could no longer squeeze into the cute little uniform the aids wore and stayed at home with Rob's parents awaiting the birth of our firstborn.

The bookkeeper left and I struggled between severe labor pains and feeling very sorry for myself. After all, other wives, or so I thought, in the wards had their husbands visiting every evening. I had my mother and Rob's mother. That was a poor substitute and I told God I didn't think it was fair.

About that time another nun came in and I recognized her as the Hospital Administrator. She smiled and held my hand. "Please don't feel badly. We so much appreciated your help when many nurses are away helping care for our soldiers. Though we hadn't begun the program you were trained for by the Red Cross you willingly came in and gave of your time and energy. Now, we have a policy that when volunteers give so much to us we want to give something back. So you will not be charged anything extra for the private room." She gave my hand a little squeeze and then left the room.

The love that woman offered me that day was all I needed to begin counting my blessings. I thanked God for sending such an angelic person to me. The blessing was really two-fold. I received love from another human being and I loved her for being so gracious. All my early childhood my grand-mother had shown such a dislike and distrust for Catholic folk that I wondered if they might not be evil. I knew without a doubt that this was a truly wonderful person and God, Himself, had sent her to minister to me.

Of course, when our son, Denny was born later that day, life became suddenly beautiful again. As I was rousing from the anesthetic, I saw the doctor holding a squalling baby boy by the heels. Besides noticing he was a boy, I noticed that he had two deep dimples in his cheeks. With every yell, the dimples went in and out. *Thank you, Lord, for giving us a child with dimples. You added that because you knew how much I have always liked dimples.*

Rick Warren in his book, *The Purpose Driven Life,* says, "Life is all about love." I am more aware of that fact as Robby and I get older and need one another for simple physical tasks.

When our four children were growing up I seemed to have more conflicts with daughter, Claudia, than the other three. She was strong willed and I was strong willed and we naturally clashed at times. I often prayed *Lord, please channel that will of hers for your glory. Help her not to be self centered but God centered as she grows.* Claudia, now grown and a mother of five, has the most compassionate heart of anyone I know. For years she has gone to the County Hospital to work with terminal patients. When her friends have suffered loss of a loved one she is always there with assistance and comfort. I know my prayers for her have been answered in ways I couldn't even imagine. God so loved that daughter of ours that He has planted in her heart a compassionate love for others. Some day God in Heaven will say to the daughter I love and He has always loved *Well done, thou good and faithful servant.*

Recently I woke suddenly one night vomiting and wrestling with diarrhea. Rob sat beside me holding a pan under my chin. The mess I made was disgusting but my dear husband cleaned me up, patted and reassured me that everything would be all right. I truly felt loved and protected that night.

Many years ago, when our son, Jerry, was a baby, he contracted whooping cough. As parents, we felt unconditional love for that baby boy. For three nights we took turns sitting up with him and holding him upright to relieve the awful coughing sieges. Although I tried to be the one with him as much as humanly possible, Rob insisted on taking turns. I know that on several occasions he must have gone to work a very weary man.

I believe God loves us beyond understanding. I also believe He arranges for us to love in ways we might not understand. I remember that when our same son, Jerry, was inducted into the Army to go to Vietnam, we were concerned for his very life. The war had gone on for too long and no mother really wanted her son to go. We never do. After he was inducted into the service in Ft. Ord, California, I received a package from the government. It contained all of Jerry's civilian clothes. As I began to unpack the box I was overcome by fear. I know that I hadn't fully placed Jerry's life and well being in God's hands. I sat down on a chair and began to cry. I just mumbled under my breath *God please take care of him*. The answer was not audible but immediate and I knew that out of God's heart came some special words to me. **Don't you think I love him more than you ever can?** God's love is great and it is certain. He always loves us and does what is best for us. We don't always recognize it as best but that is where faith and trust come in.

Soon after that the phone rang. It was my friend, Nadine. Her son, Lloyd, had gone to Vietnam earlier. She said, "Betty, I thought about Jerry this morning and knew that you would soon be receiving the box with his civilian clothes. I remember how I felt when Lloyd's clothes came. But I want you to know that God will take care of both our sons." I could hardly wait to share my experience with Nadine who had called me out of a heart of love for a friend. God really spreads His love around.

When our daughter, Jennifer, wanted to take more classes to complete her Special Education teaching credentials, I promised to keep Jonathon, her son and our grandson. He was ten months old and still in a play pen most of the time. She brought him over around two o'clock and picked him up at seven. I think that allowed her time for two classes. Jonathon could not walk yet but was a very active little boy. He could climb over and out of the play pen in a matter of moments. That meant I spent all my time watching him. When it was time for his nap, I climbed in the play pen with him and curled up there until he went to sleep. Usually Robby came home while we were both still in the play pen. He then took over and either placed Jon in his stroller for a walk around the block or drove around the neighborhood in the car. I was then free to prepare the evening meal. Neither Rob nor I resented the changes in our schedule. We loved our daughter. We knew she would be a wonderful teacher. I am convinced that God has placed in a parent's heart the kind of love He has for all of us. It is unconditional.

Jennifer became a Special Education teacher and, as I have said before, has since then been diagnosed with the progressive disease Parkinson's. We enjoyed watching Jon grow and I am reminded of two more incidents regarding that delightful grandson.

When Jon was in First Grade we accompanied Jennifer and Mike and family to church on Sunday. As Jennifer and Mike were gathering the three children to leave for home, Jon was nowhere to be found. We all searched and discovered him coming out of his empty Sunday School room. He said, "Here, Grandma and Grampa, these pencils are for you. Every one who visits our class gets one." Now, that had to be an act of love. Love of a grandson for his grandparents. God motivates that too, I'm sure.

The second incident I remember was much later. Jon was in college on a baseball scholarship. We had moved to Arizona and Jon's team was playing several teams in Phoenix. We drove the hundred miles from our home to Phoenix where the team was playing. I was experiencing some heart problems at that time and was not strong enough to sit in the bleachers for long. Robby, however, was right there rooting for his grandson. Meanwhile, I had gone back to the car to rest.

Rob came back to the car and said the game was over. He said that Jon was disappointed that I didn't get to see him play. He was determined to come say "Hello" before he and the rest of the team went on to the next game. Just then, I saw a very "sweaty" Jon, in his baseball gear come running up to our car. "Just had to say 'Hi,' sorry you couldn't stay at the game." He gave me a big hug and I was overwhelmed. The bus carrying the rest of the team had pulled up in the parking lot and Jon was being hailed, "Come on, we're gonna be late." Jon just grinned and sauntered over to the bus. This grandma's heart was bursting with pride and love. God is good!

While I'm thinking about the joys of grandparenthood I'd like to add another incident. This has to do with granddaughter Becky. We were at Claudia's for Christmas and Jennifer's family had been there but were just leaving. I looked out the window and saw Mike helping Jennifer who was awkwardly trying to get into their car. I had not seen her effort to walk for several months and did not really know the toll the Parkinson's Disease had taken on her body. It hit me. This was our baby and she could no longer bounce around as she once had. With the aid of her walker she could get around, but barely. My heart was breaking. I sat on the couch and put my head in my hands. My shoulders were shaking as I sobbed out my grief.

That was when I sensed the presence of Becky. She sat beside me, patted me on the shoulder and didn't say a word. She loved her grandmother who loved Jennifer so much. She didn't talk but I began to feel quieted and comforted. I knew at that moment that our Heavenly Father who has a heart of love was in control and He would never leave me nor forsake me. *Thank you, Becky. Thank you, Lord.*

Our families are certainly part of God's over all plan for our lives. He knows how desperately we will need comforting at times.

CHAPTER SEVEN

Getting Acquainted With God

*The Lord is my strength and song, and He has become
my salvation; this is my God, and I will praise Him; my
father's God and I will extol Him.*

Exodus 15:2

I've been thinking that if I'm going to spend an eternity
with God I'd better be well acquainted with Him. That
may sound strange. I've been a Christian for more than sixty
years. I am secure in my relationship with Christ and with
the Father. It has always been easy for me to pray. But do I
really know God? I know He is an awesome God and with
my finite mind I can never understand everything about God.
I know, as well, that God has revealed much about Himself
in His Word. That must be all I need to know.

It might be helpful to study God's character. Exodus
gives us a great deal of help here. Exodus 15:3 says that
"The Lord is a warrior." He fought the Israelites' enemies
time and again. Each of us has our own battles. If I could
only remember to step back and let God handle mine.

Exodus 15:6 tells us that "Thy right hand, O Lord, is
majestic in power..." God is majestic and powerful. When

I am weak, He is strong. That is encouraging to a weakling like me.

Exodus 15:11 reads "Who is like Thee among the gods, O Lord? Who is like Thee, majestic in holiness, awesome in praises, working wonders?" God is holy and I know the Bible tells me to be holy because of it. It makes me think twice before I step out to satisfy my own selfish and self centered desires.

Exodus 15:13 speaks of God's love, leadership and strength. "In Thy lovingkindness Thou hast led the people whom Thou hast redeemed; In Thy strength Thou hast guided them to Thy holy habitation." I am so thankful I can rely on those three characteristics because I often lack one or all of the three.

Verse 26 gives me insight into another part of God's character. "And He said, 'If you will give earnest heed to the voice of the Lord your God, and do what is right in His sight and give ear to His commandments, and keep all His statutes, I will put none of the diseases on you which I have put on the Egyptians; for I, the Lord, am your healer.'" I am grateful for the knowledge God gives to our doctors. I rely on this. But the bottom line is that God, Himself, is the healer. So when my body seems to be giving out I can, with confidence, let God do the healing or take me home to be with Him at His appointed time.

As I delved into the matter of getting to know God better, I read in John 14 that Jesus is being asked by the disciples if they can see God. Jesus answers in verse 9 "Anyone who has seen me has seen the Father." And in John 10:30 Jesus reveals "I and the Father are one." What food for thought those two statements are! Jesus Christ, God's only Son, came to earth as a baby, grew to be a man and dwelt among us. Biblical history tells us much about Jesus on earth. So now I am doing a balancing act. I thought I was being super spiritual in studying the nature and character of God the Father.

Really, I am being told to look at Christ if I want to see the Father. We know that when we are believers the Holy Spirit has come into us to help us. Jesus promised that He would never leave or forsake us. He also explained to His disciples that He, in the person of the Holy Spirit, would dwell in us. Likewise, the Holy Spirit, whom Jesus called the "Comforter" would teach and help us live the lives God intended for us to live. I don't pretend to understand how three can be one. I just know the Bible tells us that there is a godhead, made up of God the Father, Jesus Christ the Son and the Holy Spirit. This trinity had no beginning and has no end. That also is more than my mind can comprehend. But if God says it is so I accept it. I believe we will understand more later on. For now God has given us the Holy Scriptures to help us understand what He wants us to know. That is why I am going to look more closely into the life of Jesus Christ as He dwelt here on earth in order to know God the Father better.

I thought I should focus on what the Bible says about the character of God. Now, in studying scripture I find that God revealed Himself to us in the person of His Son, Jesus Christ. We must not treat that fact lightly. Jesus became a human being, like us, and much of the thirty-three years he spent here among us has been documented. I believe our responsibility is to learn as much of that documentation as we can.

The four gospels, Matthew, Mark, Luke and John clearly tell of Christ's life while on this earth. So back to the study of the gospels. Matthew is the bridge between the Old Testament and the New. How fitting that Matthew portrayed Christ in His kingly role. A king usually has complete control of his subjects. That has to be the key to knowing God's will for my relationship with Him. That is, letting Christ be in control. Letting Him make my decisions, direct my emotions, my actions. I am so quick to make my own plans. When I have been trained to do a certain job, I often try to use my own experience and expertise to complete a task. If Christ has control of my life then He decides what actions I take at any one time.

Today Robby and I went to the Mall to walk. He is so disciplined in the matter of exercise. And part of his recuperating from surgery involves exercise. I tend to get lazy and do what feels good. I do like to be comfortable. The Mall has a new pretzel shop near the food court. Some time ago, I discovered how good the special sugar cinnamon pretzels can be. When Rob has finished his walk (I do half the amount he does) we usually buy a cup of coffee and sometimes a pretzel. This was a normal day and we shared a yummy gooey pretzel.

We are planning to drive to California in June for grandson Tim's wedding. I should look for a dress to wear to the wedding. So when Rob announced he had one more round to walk I said I would meet him at Dillard's. I wanted to go through the dress racks and see if there might be a suitable dress I could buy. I was extremely happy to find that Dillard's was having a sale. One rack was marked "75% off." Now that is the kind of sale Robby would like. A friendly sales clerk helped me get settled in the fitting room to try on three dresses. One I was sure would be perfect. A beautiful suit for $20! The size was right. The color was great and I was confident. The rude awakening! I couldn't get into any of the dresses. I have gained weight. All those cakes and cookies I have been baking are now showing on me.

As I met Robby outside I said ruefully, "No more Wetzel's Pretzels." I knew the weight gain was my own fault. I have become careless and lazy. I have been doing my own thing for too long and God can't be pleased with that attitude. I am now praying *Lord, please help me to be the disciplined person you've taught me to be. After all, I truly want to represent you. How can I do that when I give in to anything that makes me feel good? I need your help.*

I know that when anything in my life is "out of control" God is not in control. I want Him to have total control. Life works better that way.

The theme of the Gospel of Mark is Christ the Servant. Mark 10:45 says "For even the Son of Man did not come to be served, but to serve, and to give His life a ransom for many. In Rick Warren's book, *The Purpose Driven Life*, he says "We serve God by serving others."

That may be a problem for many of us who would rather be served than to serve others. I know that from my childhood in poverty I met the challenge of my low position by saying, "I'm as good as anyone who has more money or fewer brothers and sisters." I grew up generating a lot of false pride. Still, I don't think I resent having been poor. I learned so many things that we really need to know later in life. Like how to live on a very meager income or how to use what I have to the best advantage.

A friend, Jeannette West, had a very different childhood. Her father was a high officer in the Army and often was in charge of an entire Army facility. Jeannette told me later that she was truly an "army brat." She was spoiled by everyone on base and grew up believing that she was a very special person who deserved everything she got. And more.

But God had plans for Jeannette and when she was middle age she became a Christian. When I knew her she loved studying Scripture and applying it to her life. She was my Administrative Assistant in the large Bible Study I taught. She confided in me one day that she was praying for "a servant's heart." She said it didn't come easy for her even though God had planted in her a love for others.

Class that year was nearly over and the large church we belonged to was planning their usual Vacation Bible School. Each year the mothers were encouraged to bring their children and stay for a special class for mothers. An experienced teacher taught the mothers and those mothers, as well as the children, benefited. Jeannette secretly was hoping she would be asked to teach. She loved to stand up in front of a crowd. However, before VBS began Jeannette was asked to help in the kitchen getting the refreshments ready for the children. Remembering her prayer that God would give her a servant's heart, Jeannette agreed to help in the kitchen.

I had to be out of town for a few days but we returned the first day of VBS. In the middle of the morning I received a frantic call from a friend. "Pray for Jeannette. She collapsed at church and is on the way to the hospital."

I immediately began to pray for my friend. Soon I received another call. "Jeannette didn't make it. She died on the way to the hospital." It was determined later that she'd had an aortic aneurysm.

Losing my friend was hard but I realized that actually she had made it. She had stepped into the Father's presence with a servant's heart. God had granted her request. Someone told me that Jeannette had come out of the kitchen with a cookie in her hand. She gasped "I can't swallow," and dropped to the floor. Another friend told me that Jeannette had always said she didn't want to get old. I think she never did.

The Gospel of Luke reveals Christ as our Savior. Luke also stresses the fact that Jesus Christ was fully human though He never sinned. Luke helps me to identify more with Christ than most of the other Gospels. Right away we are introduced to John the Baptist, his birth and life. John and Jesus were human cousins. I don't think that growing up they had much opportunity to do the things little boys do, like climb trees and have rock throwing contests. Nevertheless, John seemed to understand that this cousin of his was someone very special. As a young man John, while baptizing, told the crowds, "One is coming who is mightier than I, and I am not fit to untie the thong of His sandals; He will baptize you with the Holy Spirit and fire."

That quote speaks volumes about the young man called John the Baptist. He was not self seeking or overly proud. He also must have been walking very closely with God to receive such a message and boldly proclaim it to his followers. In fact, when Jesus had come to John and asked to be baptized, John seemed overwhelmed with the idea. As he had said before this Jesus was someone very special, "He must increase, I must decrease."

I believe Jesus must have made an impression on His cousin very early in life or perhaps John's mother, Elizabeth, had shared with her son the account of Mary's visit before either baby boy was born. At any rate, there was no rivalry between John and Jesus.

I remember what fun my brothers and sisters had with our cousins as all of us were growing up. However, there was certainly much rivalry and, often, actual dissension between us. By His example Jesus teaches us much about how to interact with our human siblings and relatives.

At the beginning of Jesus Christ's three year ministry here on earth He was tempted by Satan. We can always identify with Christ in His temptations because we so often face temptation. One thing I know — the Bible tells us that we will never be tempted more than we are able to find a way out of it. It also says that Christ was tempted in all ways as we are. What did He do about His temptations? He quoted Scripture to Satan.

When our oldest daughter, Claudia, was in High School she had a social studies class whose instructor gave the class instruction on "existentialism." He told the students that nothing really exists except in your mind. I don't know where he went with the subject but I do know that Claudia was shaken by the challenge to think differently. She had trouble sleeping at night as she tried to sort out all she had been told. One night I got up at about 12:30 to find Claudia in the living room. She told me about the class and how she hadn't been able to sleep for several nights.

Because our daughter had always been a deep thinker who liked to explore every avenue, she was naturally upset. I did not attempt to get into all the aspects of what she was being taught. I felt she was under satanic attack. I reminded her of the story from the Bible of Christ's temptations and how He dealt with them. He quoted Scripture. She was very quiet but listened to my advice. I asked her if she would memorize a page of Scripture which I would write out and then, by rote, say those verses when she had trouble sleeping. She agreed. She was tired.

For several days little was said about the late night encounter we'd had. She was a senior in High School and was applying to various colleges and universities. One particular application had a question: If up is down and down is up, where are you and what do you have? She brought me the answer she had prepared. It read: "If up is down and down is up you are nowhere and you have nothing. Life is full of absolutes and black is black and white is white." I didn't think her answer would serve to get her accepted in most of the secular universities but I was proud of her for getting out of the quagmire of thinking which had kept her awake so many nights.

Perhaps because Luke was a physician his account of Jesus' life is full of interactions. Jesus, in healing a leper, reached out and touched the man. It was almost unheard of for anyone to touch a leper. Imagine what that must have meant to the leper. His self esteem would necessarily be at an all time low. He had been forced to go about crying "Unclean." And everyone avoided him. But Jesus cared. That is a characteristic I want to have. I want to truly care about others, especially the ones other folks don't care about. God loved every one of us so much that He gave His only Son to die for us. I need to see that in order to be better acquainted with God, Himself.

Another quality that Luke highlights in his gospel is how Jesus was able to meet everyone right where they are. He related to each one on his or her level. When He healed Peter's mother-in-law He allowed her to get up and wait on the men. That was probably highly important to her. Feeling useless is one of the worst ways we can feel. As Robby and I get older and each of us has our weak and wobbly days it is important to me to be able to prepare his meals. It has always been fun for me to cook for the man I love because he is so appreciative. I have been spoiled as a wife. Some men don't appreciate their wives from the first day of marriage.

When Luke writes about Jesus raising the twelve year old girl from the dead he tells us that Jesus then gave instructions for them to bring the child something to eat. Now isn't that just what most children would want? I can almost hear her saying, "I'm hungry."

The gospel according to Luke is certainly an interpersonal account of Jesus as He interacted daily with people who came to Him. Through many of those accounts I have learned that Jesus taught us not to be jealous of what others have, to be faithful, to value our special time for prayer, and to trust our Heavenly Father for all our needs.

The gospel of John addresses the deity of Christ. We have already seen that He was fully human. At the same time He was fully God. How can that be? I don't know but I am certain the Bible tells us it is so.

I have studied and taught the gospel of John many times. Always I have felt closer to God than in any other in depth Bible study. In this book Jesus called Himself the Son of God. In fact, it was because of this the Jewish leaders wanted to kill Him. Eventually they did, of course. The identification of Jesus with His father, God, is very real. That is difficult for me to understand but I accept the fact. My understanding is up to God, Himself. I know He will, through His Holy Spirit explain what I need to know for now. Later on I will know more.

What I consider the key verse of the entire Bible is found in the gospel of John.

"For God so loved the world, that He gave His only begotten Son, that whoever believes in Him should not perish, but have eternal life." Without this promise we'd have no hope. Getting old would be truly gruesome. Instead of looking forward to a beautiful future, we would find ourselves trying to enjoy looking at the past when we had youth and stamina. And dreams for ourselves and our children. I cling to this verse because it means that I am surrounded by the love of God. I'm cared for. I have a wonderful eternity planned by God, Himself. What better future can anyone hope for?

In that same chapter is another very important verse. "Whoever believes in the Son has eternal life, but whoever rejects the Son will not see life, for God's wrath remains on him." (Or *her*) Now that quote scares me. We have grand-children and close friends who don't seem to understand this passage. Or feel it is important to their lives.

I don't like the idea of spending eternity without those loved ones. *Oh, Father, please help me to be faithful in telling others about you. I know what I read in your Word is true. Some of the others haven't discovered that yet. I pray that not one of them will be lost for eternity. Thank you for listening.*

In chapter 4 of John is a verse I find fascinating. I don't understand it fully but I am fascinated. "God is spirit, and His worshipers must worship in spirit and in truth." John 4:24.

I remember a few years ago when Rob and I were traveling in New England. We saw an old stone church with a beautiful garden adjoining. We were strolling in the garden when we saw a gentleman also strolling the garden paths. He was smoking a huge pipe. I whispered to Robby that I hoped that wasn't the pastor. He didn't look very spiritual to me. On Sunday we decided to attend the church we had visited.

That evening after going to bed I prayed, "Dear Lord, help me tomorrow to worship you in spirit and in truth." I still didn't quite understand what that meant even though I had read it in the Scriptures.

That Sunday was a beautiful, sunny day. No one spoke to us and I was ready to make an unkind mental evaluation of the place. I thought *This place is as cold as the stones it's made of.* Then I remembered my prayer of the night before. *I want to worship you in spirit and in truth.*

Sure enough, the clergy who stood up to lead the service was the man we had seen in the garden the day before. *Help me, Lord, to worship you in spirit and in truth.*

I don't remember a word of the man's sermon but I <u>do</u> remember how I felt that morning and all through the day. I sensed God's presence as never before. The service was not long but in some way I was transported to new heights. I was glad to be in God's house, worshiping my Father in spirit and in truth.

That experience has helped me tremendously to realize I don't have to understand everything. God knows it all. I can trust Him and I intend to do that for the rest of my life, be that for a long time or not so long. I can rejoice in the fact that He is continually teaching me new things—about myself, about others, about Him.

CHAPTER EIGHT

Immortality

In the way of righteousness is life, and in its pathway there is no death.

Proverbs 12:28 (NAS)

If you've seen the stage play *Evita*, you know the story is about Eva Peron, the wife of Argentina's president, Juan Peron. The self-centered woman was obsessed with her own beauty and immortality. Of course we know now she didn't live forever. On this earth anyway. The Bible tells us that everyone will live forever, either in eternity with God our maker or damned and punished forever. That is reason enough to cause anyone to want to know more about what it means to live forever with God.

Jesus Christ made it possible for us to do that when He died for our sins. I find it hard to understand why there are so many people in the world today who ignore or scoff at anything the Bible says. Now that I am old I find great solace in the fact that I have a wonderful forever just waiting for me. I am very concerned that some of the folks I know and love don't have that assurance.

Grandchildren are especially important to me. They are God's gift to mankind, after all. The memories Robby and I have of each of our twelve grandchildren could fill twelve books. Now we enjoy recounting some of those memories to one another.

Geoffrey, you were the first and we were certain no one had a better looking or smarter grandson than we had. No wonder. Just look at the parents you have. We still are proud of you though we can't see you often. We pray for you now as a man and father. We want you to teach your son the truths you learned at home. We want you to know the same Savior we know so all of us can be together in eternity. We wish we had lived close enough to get to know Jenni. She is a wonderful wife and mother, we're sure. Perhaps she already has the assurance of her eternity.

Then, Chris, you came along and we had to shift our opinion that only one super grandson existed. We now had two and none of our peers could outdo us with the stories that were told about grandchildren. We loved to watch the cousin rivalry as both of you grew. We found it was possible to love both of you equally as we always had our four children. All are so different but so special. Maybe that is why we pray always for you, and Hiroko too, that you will be with us forever. God knows your hearts.

That cousin rivalry showed quite often in subtle ways. Both boys wanted a baby sister and Geoff often added a prayer for one when his Mom tucked him in at night. But, alas, God sent Chris a baby sister first. And he hadn't even prayed for one. We thought we heard Geoff grumble that one day.

Our third grandchild was the cutest little girl we'd ever seen. True she had a strong will and a mind of her own but that made her even more adorable. We watched you, Tina, as you developed into a determined child who loved pretend tea parties and new clothes. I remember particularly one day when you asked me to pretend with you. You said, "I'll be the grown up and you be four years old." That worked for a few minutes but you soon needed a drink of water and help with a bathroom trip. We switched back to being us. You had a brilliant mind for a child. Just ask grandma and grandpa. When you were a little older, you memorized blocks of scripture. In fact, both Grandpa and I said you put us older folk to shame.

We loved you then and we love you now, Tina. Our prayer is that you recall some of that scripture you memorized as a child and choose Jesus to be your Savior. We can't bear thinking of an eternity without you. We pray the same for Ben, though distance has made it impossible for us to know him well. God knows him and loves him too. We know that for sure.

Next, Mark, you came on the scene. At a very early age you were fascinated with words. I remember once when we were babysitting you for a weekend. I read an animal book to you and pointed out the various animals. When I said "dog" you repeated "dog."

You knew the more familiar animals but we came to a picture of an elephant. You had no experience with that animal. I read "elephant." You repeated "elephant." Later, after we had turned out the light and stood in the hallway we heard you saying over and over "elephant," "elephant." I think you enjoyed saying three syllables. When you were a bit older and attended Bible study with your Mom, you remembered everything the children's leaders said and repeated them at home.

Perhaps when they explained that Jesus loves you and is your best friend if you want Him to be, you weighed those words. You just have to invite Him into your heart and He promises to come in and live with you. You shared some of that with your Mom also. We are praying now that, as a father to precious Thomas, you will share the truths you learned as a very little boy. Sometimes we wish we hadn't moved so far away so we could know the spouses of our grandchildren. We try to make up for it by praying faithfully for our young mothers. Tiffany is very wise and Thomas is fortunate to have both of you for parents. Please plan to spend eternity with us. Then we can really get better acquainted.

Susan, you came along next. Geoffrey's prayers were finally answered. He had a little sister and we had another granddaughter. When we babysat you and Geoff, (you both were in school) I was as likely as not to find you upside down on the bars when I picked you up at school. You were so active almost from birth I think. You were also a very thoughtful young lady. I remember one Sunday we were on our way home from church and you were sitting on my lap. We didn't have many car seats for kids then. Anyway, I told Grandpa that some parents were going to hate me because of a change the committee I chaired had made in the children's church.

You commented, "Jesus doesn't want us to hate anyone." You had learned your Sunday School lessons well. I'm sure you accepted what you were taught and at an early age chose Jesus to take charge of your life. Because of that and later decisions we expect to spend eternity with you. What a beautiful future God has planned for you. And us.

Next, another delightful grandson came along. Eric, we loved your red hair and the way you seemed to know how to do anything mechanical. When you saw our new exercise bike you crawled all around it. You were puzzled because it only had one wheel. You announced, finally, "I think my Daddy could fix that."

Later, when you were older and attending church camp, you became very serious about your spiritual self. I somehow obtained a letter you had written to God. You really wanted Him in your life. We trust you still feel that way. Because, you see, we really want you with us in the beautiful forever God has promised all who believe in Him and His Son, Jesus.

God was so good to give us an abundance of grandsons. We were truly blessed when Timothy was born. You were a considerate and kind little boy who had a marvelous sense of humor. We suspected early on that a child like you could grow up to serve God. And you have. We pray often for your ministry and your future. Now, with a precious wife beside you even more young people, and others, can be reached for Christ. We'd like to know Mariah better but with a whole eternity waiting for us we can get well acquainted. And she can get to know us better. It's good to know that life on this earth is not all there is for us.

The next grandson God gave us was Brian. What a treasure! We soon knew that you were very intelligent. By this time we had become experts in determining things like that. At times you were so far ahead of your peers that we were amazed. For instance, at a birthday party where fried chicken was served you explained to the boys and girls some of the elements of bone marrow. We wondered about your social skills. People don't like to look stupid and some of the kids might have felt that way when they tried to figure out what you were talking about.

We didn't need to worry. You soon learned the importance of relationships and went about developing friendships. When you decided to major in archaeology we knew that would be a subject tailored to your personality. Then when you settled on cultural archaeology, the matter of relationships was also settled. You like people and want to know as much about them as possible. Relationships are important to you and we know that God planted that characteristic in you. Now, we are trusting that your relationship with God, Himself, is right and that we get to be forever with you.

The next special grandson was Brian's cousin, Jonathon. What an active little boy you were, Jon! Considerate too. We always remember how you gave us the Sunday School guest pencils. As your grandmother, I think the incident I have already described in this book is most outstanding. That is, when you made a special effort to see your ailing grandparent after a baseball game. You can't know how much that meant to me and how the incident will always be in my memory bank. That may be one of the reasons that we want you to be always with us in the next segment of our lives. **Eternity.**

We loved having all those grandsons, but now it was time for another granddaughter. Apparently God felt the same way because He gave Claudia and Gary a beautiful little girl. They named her Rebekah. Everyone calls her "Becky," and that just fits. As for your grandmother, Becky, you were everything I could wish for. You let me teach you to do crafts of all kinds. When you grew up and went to college I remember thinking that you would have so many other interests that you couldn't have time for me. I shoudn't have worried. You, as an adult, have proved that you have a loving heart of compassion and have always been around for Grandma and Grandpa. We love you so much and want to spend a wonderful forever with you. That can be arranged if you choose to believe in the same Jesus we do. We think you have and look forward to an eternity getting to know you even better.

Kimberly, "destiny's child," or more correctly, "part of God's plan," you came next. You rounded out a perfect set of granddaughters. Now, each of our children had a daughter, and we had four beautiful granddaughters.

When you were very young, in some ways you reminded us of Tina. You were strong willed and struggled to be independent.

Some time ago, your mother tearfully commented, "Kim has had an ailing mother most of her life. It just isn't fair." We know it has to be hard. We also know it has made you a stronger, more caring person. God trusts persons He loves with hardships. Sometimes I wish it weren't so. I don't want those I love to suffer, but often they do. And part of God's plan is that they become more like Jesus in order to spend an eternity with Him. Grandpa and I plan to ask Jesus how all that works when we get to Heaven. We want you there with us when He gives us some answers. On the other hand, maybe I don't need all the answers. Being forever with our Savior may be all any of us really needs.

Then there was Will. You made the number even and we know that twelve grandchildren is just what God planned for us all along. As you grow to maturity we know you are developing into the person God intended you to be. We love you and want you with us always. It is exciting to hear of the many church activities in which you are involved. So long as you keep focused on God's will for your life, we are confident you will be with us always.

Now, to all of you who read this book, you've met our grandchildren. I'm sure you sense how much we wish to see all of them in Heaven with us some day. I pray that each of you, dear readers, will also consider God's great plan for your life and choose the immortality we can have in God's Presence. As I have said before, that will come about only if you choose to make Jesus Christ your Savior.

CHAPTER NINE

Eternal Choices

*And if it seem evil unto you to serve the Lord, choose you
this day whom ye will serve; whether the gods which your
fathers served that were on the other side of the flood, or
the gods of the Amorites, in whose land ye dwell: but as for
me and my house, we will serve the Lord.*

Joshua 14:15 (KJV)

L ife is full of choices. As little children we often make
wrong choices. As we mature and are better able to
make right choices we need to be so committed to God's
purpose for our lives that we automatically know what is
right and what is wrong. The reason that is possible is that we
are promised that the Holy Spirit lives in us prompting and
guiding us. He does what Jesus would do. This message is to
those who have already chosen Jesus to be their Savior.

I have a friend who is happily married to a fine Christian
man. It was not always so. She explains that as a young
person she made many wrong choices. Her life was one of
self centered attempts to have fun, do only what she wanted
to do and generally go the way of the world. She experienced
a life of abuse from men. Eventually, she met and married

her present husband. He was considerate, kind and loving. The husband brought four children into the marriage. My friend had three. For a time the two of them pursued the same life style both of them had been in. They were good parents to their large blended family, but neither of them had met Jesus.

God had great plans for this couple and they one day became believers in Jesus Christ. Their lives were never the same after that. My friend's oldest daughter became a Christian and was determined that her parents should follow. They did. I have never seen a couple more devoted to the Lord and His will for their lives. Though they may have made some wrong choices before, they certainly made the right one for eternity. They are committed to serve Jesus.

Randy Alcorn, in his little book, *In the Light of Eternity,* states that God cares a great deal about our lives now and says, "...the door of eternity swings on the hinges of choices made here and now." He has reached the conclusion that choices we make while alive on this earth are significant in the next segment of our lives, eternity.

The Bible tells us that we must send on ahead of us building materials that will last. I Corinthians 3:11-13 says that God will test all the things we've done, the choices we've made while alive on earth. The works which God has chosen for us to do, as well as the choices we have made, will remain for eternity. Also, we will be rewarded for them. The others, those works and choices, which we accomplish on our own will be destroyed.

Because we are promised that the Holy Spirit will conform all believers to the image of Jesus Christ, we know that conformation is not complete so long as we live here on earth. Along the way we make many immature choices. As parents, however, we are expected to help our children make the right choices.

When Claudia was very young, probably six or seven, she disliked very much going to the dentist. I can appreciate that. At 84 years of age I still dislike visiting the dentist. Nonetheless, I have learned that some things need to be done. One day I planned to take Claudia to our children's dentist for a necessary visit. When it was time to leave home, I couldn't find Claudia. She had hidden under the bed. I looked under there and announced, "Come on out. It is time to go." Claudia answered, "I'm not coming out. I'm not going. Even if you kill me, I'm not coming out."

Her determined answer surprised me. We didn't beat or mistreat our children. In fact, we loved our children very much and made every effort to assure them of that. So I needed to supersede that childish declaration in a loving way. I merely answered, "I'm going to get the car out of the garage. Don't keep me waiting or we will be late."

Then I added, "Your teeth are very healthy and beautiful. We just want to keep them that way."

I left the room and backed the car out of the garage. Claudia was standing on the front porch waiting for me. I wonder if God sometimes looks at each of us and thinks, "She, or he, is not making a wise choice. I have promised to take care of my children and must make the better choice." Perhaps that is why some of our prayers aren't answered just the way we think they should be. We don't realize we are making immature requests. Romans 8:28 is our assurance that God is always watching out for us. "And we know that God causes all things to work together for good to those who love God, to those who are called according to His purpose."

There have been a number of TV commercials recently depicting grown people doing extremely stupid things. For instance, a young man steps onto a moving treadmill at a rakish angle and immediately lands on his back. There are several other scenarios showing that folks often make bad choices. Folks that should know better. I can't even remember now what the commercials are advertising but the fact is there. You and I aren't always as wise as we should be. In the book of James in the Bible we read, "If any of you lacks wisdom, let him ask of God, who gives to all men generously and without reproach, and it will be given to him." It would seem to me that there is no reason for a Christian to make bad choices when God has made so great an offer to all His children.

We tend to make choices within the framework of the personality God has given each of us. For instance, I think with my heart instead of my head. Sometimes I do things on impulse. Once, when I was teaching Bible Study Fellowship, a class member presented me with a beautiful orchid corsage. The class members knew how much I enjoyed flowers and each week gave me a fragrant rose or other flower, often in the form of a corsage. I was proud to display the flowers on my lapel or on the pulpit while I gave the morning lecture.

After class some of us went to a Christian book store across the street from the church. We had discovered that one of the clerks was uncooperative and grumpy most of the time. On this particular day, I spoke when we went inside and she mumbled some answer. As I noted that she had on a dress the same color as the one I was wearing, I thought *She might like someone to give her a corsage.* Without thinking further, I unpinned the corsage and asked her if I could pin it on her. She smiled and I'm sure she had tears in her eyes as she said yes, she would like that very much. From that day on, none of us ever saw her in a grumpy or unfriendly mood. I never did get to know the woman more than casually but I was certain God had prompted me to do something nice for her. She probably just needed a simple touch of kindness.

Now, on the other hand, my engineer husband is seldom compulsive but almost always logical. When he first retired from work he planned that he would take over the book-keeping of our income. He keeps a spread sheet noting every penny we spend and what we have spent it for. At the end of the year we have a perfect record of our income and our spending. The other day I talked him into buying two dress shirts on sale. He was happy they were on sale but, nonetheless, had to justify buying two. He agreed, "All right, one is my Father's Day gift and the other my birthday gift."

When we decided to sell our travel trailer, a niece and nephew wanted to buy it but didn't have enough money for the full price. Robby set up a payment plan, and they paid it off in about two years. The last payment was to be made in December. Robby asked me if I thought it would be all right to excuse that last payment. These parents have three boys and would need extra money for Christmas gifts. Of course I liked the idea.

While Robby and I have different personalities, we look to the same source for our decisions. The Holy Spirit prompts each of us to make mature choices. We are still growing into Christ's image, though, and either of us can leap into making immature choices. That is why we need to pray about everything.

In the book of Genesis we read how God made man and woman in the image of the Godhead. It is somewhat of a mystery what is meant by that but I believe part of the meaning is that, like God, we have free choice. We can decide to obey God or go our own ways. When God made the animals, birds and fish, He let Adam choose names for them. Later on, He gave both Adam and Eve the privilege of choosing whether or not to obey Him. As you know, they disobeyed and mankind has suffered and Jesus had to die as a result of the bad choices of our ancient ancestor.

As I have thought about the reasons we make the choices we do, I spoke about the differences in our personality. God has given us sufficient help, however, to make right choices. One thing that helps is having the right mindset. In Daniel

1:8 we are told that "Daniel made up his mind that he would not defile himself. . ." Later, Daniel is visited by an angel who says, "Do not be afraid, Daniel, for from the first day that you set your heart on understanding. . ." As a young man Daniel, through no choice of his own, had been abducted and carried from his home. He chose to remain the believer and follower of the God of his youth.

In the book of Mark, Jesus rebukes Peter for not choosing to believe Him. Fortunately, Jesus places the blame where it belongs, on Satan. He said "Get behind Me, Satan; for you are not setting your mind on God's interests, but man's." That should tell us where the wrong choices originate. It should also encourage us to live closer to Christ each day of our lives.

In my Bible I have underlined Romans 8:5-8. It reads, "For those who are according to the flesh set their minds on the things of the flesh, but those who are according to the Spirit, the things of the Spirit.

"For the mind set on the flesh is death, but the mind set on the Spirit is life and peace, because the mind set on the flesh is hostile toward God; for it does not subject itself to the law of God, for it is not even able to do so; and those who are in the flesh cannot please God."

We get to choose which camp we want to be in. God welcomes all believers into the Kingdom as His own children. That, to me, is an exciting place to be.

I doubt that a little baby actually makes a conscious choice whether to cry or not. He soon discovers that he can get the attention his little being desires by certain actions. Most of the choices concerning a newborn infant are the responsibility of the mother and father and others around that child.

Most of a child's demands are centered around himself. He needs to be taught by others that the world does not revolve around him. I remember that in the early life of each of our four children, Robby and I would have sacrificed almost anything to assure their comfort and safety. The choices we made were not selfish. We loved them too much for that. Later on, the choices we made concerning them were still because we loved them, just as we do today. When Jerry would plead for a pony, the choice we made was easy, based on the knowledge we had as adults. We could not keep a pony in our yard in the city. Jerry, in his immaturity, argued that he would do all the work and figure out how to get enough hay to feed the animal.

When three year old Denny walked into the middle of the street following a school band, I knew immediate discipline was called for. He should never do such a dangerous thing again. I knew that. He didn't know there was any danger. Or even what the word meant.

Before we were married, Robby and I had many choices to make. I'll admit I didn't do much praying about whether or not to get married. Rob knew that he wanted a wife, and that wife had to be ME. I think I was eager to get away from home and the little town of Concordia. Robby was not a Christian at that time and I had not learned what the Bible said about being "unequally yoked."

Robby as a boy had been baptized in a watering tank for livestock and assumed that he was a Christian also. He learned later from Scripture that he had to make a personal commitment.

He tells of a time he discovered that he was not really a Christian because he didn't have a personal relationship with Jesus Christ. He had assumed too much because he had been baptized as a boy. He prayed that night that God would accept him into His family and forgive his sins. From that time on we were believers together. For years I had prayed that my husband would become the spiritual head of the family and that prayer was now answered.

The earlier choice he had made to ask me to marry him was one which could have gone very wrong. My assumption that he was a believer was not a good one, of course. Sometimes, I am thankful to say, God intervenes in our poor choices and the results are good. This was one of those times. I'm glad that our Heavenly Father looked down on his foolish children and chose not to punish them for their ignorance. Robby has been the spiritual leader in our family for many years. I know we will be in Heaven together some day. There is still much to be discovered about relationships in Heaven. I puzzle over the fact that we won't be married in Heaven. We certainly will be together as joint heirs of Christ and God's children. That will be one great family gathering!

I asked Rob to try to recall some of the poor choices he had made in the past. He is always so logical and mentioned a time after World War II. It had been impossible to get new automobiles during the war. It was possible, however, at the end of the war to order a new car and be one of the first to receive one when normal production started. Rob's father offered to make the down payment on one for us. We would pay him back later. Before my husband came home, though, he began to worry about our finances and asked me to have his father cancel the order. My father-in-law was not very happy but agreed. After Robby came home we had difficult days without an automobile and it was a long time before we could buy a new one. That, looking back, Rob says, was a bad choice.

I can recall some of the choices and decisions I made in bringing up our children which were certainly not the best. In retrospect I know I did not pray before I acted and that can never be good. God has forgiven each wrong thing I did as I have confessed it to Him. The Holy Spirit is faithful to point out our shortcomings and then we need to make them right.

The most important decision either of us has made, however, is the one we have made for all of eternity. Both Robby and I have chosen to make Jesus Christ our Savior.

CHAPTER TEN

New Bodies

*And not only this, but also we ourselves, having the
first fruits of the Spirit, even we ourselves groan within
ourselves, waiting eagerly for our adoption as sons, the
redemption of our body.*

Romans 8:23 (NAS)

This verse of Scripture is filled with meaning. We need
to take it apart and study various phrases separately and
then put the whole thing together. Even then, there seems
to be a mystery associated with the meaning. Ryrie, in his
explanatory note on this verse, says "The culmination of our
position as adopted sons is the resurrection state." I don't get
much help from that statement. Perhaps I need to dissect the
verse and then come to a conclusion.

Beginning with the phrase *and not only this,* I find it
necessary to see what Paul is referring to, or what has gone
before. Verse 22 reads *For we know that the whole creation
groans and suffers the pains of childbirth together until now.*
When we look around us at the world today we see pain and
suffering. We also see an earth that is growing old and deteriorating in many ways. Some of that deterioration we have

brought on ourselves, of course. It is so sad to see a beautiful landscape strewn with trash. On one of our highways we noticed that local people had picked up many bags of trash. Weeks later, those same bags are still lying beside the road. No follow up on the clean up.

Also, in addition to our environment being spoiled, mankind is deteriorating due to disease and old age. No one can escape the ravages of either. So I can understand how the creature as well as the creation which once was created perfect now is in a state of disarray. It is painful to see.

But why did Paul say *until now*? I think he is saying that Christ's death on the cross gave us new hope and new life.

I want to examine *first fruits of the Spirit*. What does that mean? If it is the position we believers have, we should understand what it means. In the Old Testament the faithful were expected to bring as an offering to God the first of their harvest. There is a reason for that. They were being trained to realize that God should have the "cream of the crop." Not just the left overs. Actually, it means "putting God first." In Wycliffe's Bible Commentary we read, "First fruits here may mean the blessings and changes that the Spirit has already produced in the lives of believers." Wycliffe goes on to say "the adoption for which the believer awaits refers to the redemption of our body, its release from sin and finiteness, the pressure of which we constantly feel as long as we have our mortal body." Revelation 1:5 reads: ..."and from Jesus Christ, who is the faithful witness, the firstborn from the dead..." I believe there is a correlation of "first fruits" and "firstborn from the dead". In the footnote of Revelation 1:5 (NIV Life Application Bible) we read: "Others had risen from the dead—people whom the prophets, Jesus, and the apostles had brought back to life during their ministries—but later those people died again. Jesus was the first who rose from the dead in an imperishable body (I Corinthians 15:20), never to die again. He is the firstborn from the dead."

Robby and I can relate to the "groaning" mentioned when sometimes we feel physically drained. Most of this is caused by age, of course, and that is all part of living this segment of our lives.

Recently we drove to Southern California to attend grandson Tim's wedding. It was our first outing since Robby's open heart surgery in January. He was certain he was strong enough now to make the trip. Actually, by stopping frequently he did very well with the driving. Thank the Lord healing of Rob's body has progressed extremely well!

We had not seen Jennifer for months and were not prepared emotionally for how her Parkinson's had progressed. As the mother of the groom, she wanted desperately to walk down that center aisle on husband Mike's arm. That was not to be. Her balance is very bad now and she has to rely on a wheel chair. Tim chose to push her down the center aisle with Mike accompanying them. We had been instructed to sit on the front row beside Mike and Jennifer.

Before the wedding I peeked in the brides' room to meet Tim's fiancée and give Jennifer a hug. Our daughter was beautiful! She always has been, of course. She asked us to pray for her. The parents of both bride and groom would be giving a little speech. She confided in me that her disease had recently caused her speech to be slurred. I conveyed her request to Robby and both of us were praying silently as we sat down.

Soon, as we looked back, we saw Tim pushing his mother down the center aisle with Mike following. Claudia and her family were seated further back from us and as the threesome proceeded down the center aisle Claudia began to sob. She said she lost control and was crying audibly. Here was her sister who had always been so active. She was a cheerleader both in High School and college. Claudia said she knew the people around her were thinking, "That crazy woman. The wedding hasn't even started."

She told us that she looked at Denny, the big brother, who was sitting in the row ahead and tears were flowing down his cheeks. I'm sure that the other brother, Jerry, back a few rows, might have been stoic but was certainly crying inside. Meantime, I was trying not to cry and looked up at my wonderful husband. Tears were escaping there too. This is where we are, groaning within ourselves, but knowing there is hope for a better tomorrow. As Robby and I continued praying, we saw that Jennifer, with the help of a walker, was standing beside Mike and reading her "speech." Each parent had been asked to give a symbolic gift to the couple. Jennifer's consisted of a pillow she had made. It had a heart in the middle with Tim and Mariah's names on it. The story Jennifer gave was that as a little boy Tim had carried a special little pillow his great grandma had made. That was his "security blanket." He probably still owns a small shred of that pillow. She spoke of how his and Mariah's security rested in Jesus and they would never lack for guidance if they put their trust in Him.

Both Rob and I were happy to hear our prayers being answered as Jennifer spoke clearly and forcefully. We couldn't help thinking, however, of the hope that our youngest has in a future when she will have a "new body."

Joni Eareckson Tada in her book on Heaven speaks of hope in a future without a wheelchair. She will again be able to move about freely. For now, though, we see how God has used Joni's disability to help many others around the world.

Jennifer, too, has been used to help many children with learning disabilities. I'm sure her disease has made her a better teacher. I'd never choose this course for her, but I'm convinced God knows what is best.

Today is not a "good" day for either my husband or me. I woke this morning with chest pains but they left as soon as I sat up. Robby is so faithful to get up early, take Misty out and bring me toast and coffee in bed.

I still feel extremely tired and Rob says he isn't doing well. We plan to take a thirty minute walk, though. Misty is insisting on it.

For all the years the children were home we insisted on everyone sitting down for a wholesome breakfast. In those days, of course, I was up early doing all the things a mother does to send her family off properly. With the four children being spread out age wise, breakfast was sometimes the only meal that all of us were home at the same time. Later in the day the boys had football practice or church youth activities. Often they chose to settle for "meals on the run." For much of the time both Rob and I were working and sometimes overtime interfered with family time. So when Robby and I retired from work he proposed that I, not a "morning" person by nature, stay in bed while he brought coffee and toast to help me start the day. I love the arrangement.

While Rob was recuperating from the open heart surgery in January I asked him to let me do the early morning things for awhile. He agreed but is now much stronger and wants to get back to our old schedule. Who am I to argue about his self image? As I started to say, we are both a bit "puny" today. Age has a lot to do with it I'm sure but since we are both heart patients we are taking it easy.

Now if I can just get the laundry finished, I won't feel guilty about taking a lazy day. The inactivity, though, set me thinking again about the next segment of our lives, that is, eternity. Am I prepared for that? What am I clinging to right now? I believe I struggle more to keep my "comfort zone" intact than for anything else. I seem to require everything around me to be just right, the room temperature, the pantry and refrigerator well stocked, furniture that fits, enough sleep. Even that laundry I have started. Does it have to be completed today? I think a little more time studying and memorizing Scripture would be most useful. The Bible says that all things will pass away but God's word will not pass away. Also, spending more time in prayer for our loved ones is absolutely necessary.

I was reading an account of Joni's from her book *When God Weeps*. She tells an incident that happened in Africa when her group of friends was delivering wheelchairs to some very poor people who lived on the street. She said an eighty year old man with no legs extended a stump of an arm and she pressed her paralyzed fingers against his stump for a strange handshake. Don't you think that man, as well as Joni, will be very happy with new and perfect bodies?

When Rob and I were working with the volunteer association, MMAP, we enjoyed particularly being assigned to Rainbow Acres, a ranch providing homes for mentally handicapped adults. Most of the ranchers are of biological ages from twenty-one to sixty-five. Their mental abilities, however, are more like ten or twelve year olds. I remember, especially, one of the Ranchers whom I will call "Debbie." Debbie had such a problem with her emotions that she screamed and threw things probably to the extent of being a danger to her fellow ranchers as well as herself. The ranch authorities were giving her one more chance to cooperate or her folks would have to remove her from the facility.

She was amiable much of the time. The MMAPers were able to talk with Debbie and all of us tried to be as friendly as possible. She and I were having a little discussion one day as we sat on a bench in the yard.

She said, "You know, I'm really looking forward to getting to Heaven. The Bible says I will get a new body and that means I will get a new brain. I will be able to think straight and not get into trouble all the time. Won't that be great?"

The ranch staff did have to ask Debbie's parents to make other arrangements for their handicapped child. We did not hear anything further but hope that the doctors were able to adjust Debbie's medications in such a way that she could interact with other people the rest of her natural life on this earth. I look forward to seeing her in Heaven some time and we can have a great conversation. Debbie will have a mind that is perfect and I will have a young and active body again.

Another MMAP project took place in Wisconsin at a large, spread out residence for physically handicapped adults. Some of the lady MMAPers had been asked to lead a morning devotion for any residents who cared to attend. I remember one pretty young girl named "Mary Ann." Mary Ann was an inspiration to everyone with her pleasant smile and friendly manner. She traveled about in a wheelchair, as did many of the residents. Mary Ann shared one morning that she had been born with spina bifada. She was the daughter of a minister and had always experienced much love and attention in her "growing-up" years.

She said that from the time she was old enough to pray she had asked God to heal her of her condition. She was extremely unhappy when her condition became worse instead of better. She said that, in desperation, one day she prayed, *Oh God, I am your child. I give you my spina bifada. Do with it what you will. Thank you for loving me.* What God did was use her quiet, gentle spirit to encourage others.

From that moment on, she never again asked for healing while she lives on this earth. She is certain God knows best and will give her a new body in the future. Mary Ann is another of the precious individuals I shall enjoy visiting with in Heaven. She will no longer have a bent and hurting body. She will probably be dancing circles around all of us, perhaps holding hands with Joni and our Jennifer.

At that same work project we found that a seminar was being held for disabled people. One evening when we MMAPers were settled in for a restful evening of watching television, meeting with others for games or just relaxing, Robby and I heard singing from across the way where the facility had a large meeting room.

After awhile we looked out the window of our motor home and saw that the meeting must have finished because a great number of folks in wheel chairs or walking with white canes were streaming out of the building. Someone began to sing and others joined in. The singing picked up in volume and we recognized the words. "When the Saints Go Marching In." Well, what do you know? Those disabled people were rejoicing because in their minds they were not disabled at all. Perhaps they were looking forward to God's promise that in the future all of them would have new bodies. I thought about the fact that there will be no need for white canes or wheel chairs in heaven.

CHAPTER ELEVEN

God's Plan

Thine eyes have seen my unformed substance; and in Thy book they were all written, the days that were ordained for me, when as yet there was not one of them.

Psalm 139:16 (NAS)

We had complained a bit because the cardiologist had not seen Robby since his surgery. I'm sure he had gone over his files. However, Rob had a stress test given by the cardiologist's assistant and which she was supposed to send to the rehab center so that rehab could begin. The office lost the test results and time went on. It had been eight months since the bypass heart surgery in Phoenix.

As we drove home from church Robby told me he had decided that he didn't need the rehab anyway. He felt fine and was on a twice a day walking regimen which strengthened his legs, heart and stamina. I agreed with him. Why bother now with driving into Prescott three times a week for rehab? We continued our conversation as we stopped for a late breakfast at Coco's.

"You know, honey," Rob began "I think that since I do so well driving we should take a trip to Kansas. We could also make a loop and go to Colorado to see my sister." I thought the idea was great and we went on planning different aspects of the trip.

I reminded my husband that we would be driving in to Prescott the next day for a memorial service for a friend from Sunday School who had died. The friend was ready to go to Heaven after a lengthy illness.

The next day as we drove in to Prescott for the service, Robby confided in me that he didn't get much sleep Sunday night. He said that he had chest pains. He had not experienced chest pains since his heart surgery in January. I asked him why he had not awakened me. He replied, "Oh they didn't last long and I didn't think it was necessary."

"How long?"

"Only about twenty or thirty minutes."

Of course I was appalled. That is too long. On being assured that he felt fine now I tried to relax but couldn't help praying that God would take control. When we got to the service we met the family of the deceased man. The service was simple and everyone was asked to remain afterwards for cake and coffee or iced tea. We sat around tables and visited with friends. I told a lady sitting next to me about Rob's story. She told me not to take it lightly because it could be a serious indication.

As we drove home I brought up the subject again and Robby said we would stop at our Primary Care doctor's office and arrange for an EKG. When he went in, the office staff took him immediately for an EKG. That test was fairly normal but because he had heart surgery in January, Dr. Gale told him he was admitting him in to the hospital for tests. Rob insisted we go home first to change clothes and, then, back to Prescott we went.

Both of us forgot our conversation about taking a vacation in Kansas. As Robert Burns said *The best laid schemes o' mice and men gang aft a-gley.* Being far removed from

Scotland I am more comfortable quoting this passage as *The best laid plans of mice and men are often gone awry.* We wanted to plan a trip to Kansas. God had other plans.

My chief concern was that Robby get the immediate medical attention he needed. Dr. Gale had called ahead and the hospital already had assigned a room to Rob. I waited until the nurses had him in bed and then went in to visit for a few minutes before driving home. Reluctantly, I kissed Robby "goodnight" and then left for home. I knew our little terrier, Misty, would be waiting and wondering where we were. Do dogs think? We sometimes feel certain ours does. I usually avoid driving after dark but, in this instance, I had no choice. It was slightly past midnight.

We have wonderful neighbors next door. I had called them after we arrived at the hospital and they were glad to go in and feed Misty as well as take her out for her short walks and potty breaks. That is a really good neighbor, don't you think?

As I drove home, I prayed *Father, please take care of my husband and help him recover from whatever is wrong. If the arteries are blocked you already know about that. You know, also, that Robby has often prayed that you would let him live as long as he needed to care for me. I just can't pump gas—or perhaps I only think I can't. How many people have offered to teach me? It certainly is going to be lonely sleeping in that big bed without the man I love and have been married to for sixty-three (nearly sixty-four) years. Forgive me, Lord, for being so selfish.*

That whole week was crammed with test after test. From one test, Dr. Gale felt that there was blockage in one artery. By the end of the week Dr. Rothrock, the cardiologist, arranged for an angiogram. Good news. The angiogram showed there was no blockage and both doctors said he could go home the next day, a Saturday. When we arrived home Misty was so glad to see her master. I was glad to have Rob sleeping beside me again. Sunday morning Rob wanted to go to church but I felt he should rest. It had been a difficult week. So I was able to convince my husband that both of us could use the rest and we stayed home all day. Toward evening, however, Robby was complaining that he didn't really feel well. I took his temperature. It was above normal, about 102. We waited awhile and took it again. It was nearly 104.

He didn't want me to call 911 but agreed I could drive him in to E.R. at the hospital. The triage nurse took his temperature and it had dropped slightly but she felt an E.R. doctor should see him. The doctor was certain Robby had an infection and needed to stay hospitalized. He spent two nights in ICU and, when stabilized somewhat the doctors decided he could be transferred to a private room. Another week of uncertainty and much prayer. All this time the medical team had my husband on heavy IV doses of antibiotics. Finally it was decided he could safely go home again but would need to stay on antibiotics. We drove in to Prescott every day for the next week for a session in the IV Therapy department. One good thing about these sessions is that we often met people worse off than Robby. We realized how blessed we are, after all.

This time of concern and uncertainty gave me lots of time to think back over our lives, or particularly mine. When I was a girl in High School and marriage was only a dream, I often made plans. Some of them came to fruition, some did not. I remember, especially, wanting a part in the play *Little Women* which our class would be presenting to all of the town. Sometimes I wonder why someone so shy and poor would even want to be in the limelight. I was always afraid to stand up in front of people. But, for some reason, I was certain I could do this.

This was my chance to be somebody. All the social snobs will sit up and take notice. Maybe I'll even get to become a famous movie star. As when I was a small child, I could go on imagining things forever.

All weekend I prayed that God would give me the part. Already I was imagining how the costumes would look. I'd seen pictures in a book. My imagination embellished the pictures and I even practiced swishing around in a long gown. I wanted the part of Jo. So far as being the oldest in the family and a bit bossy, the character was really a part of my life. If I lived it, I could also portray it, I felt. Of course my motives were all wrong. I wanted the part for selfish reasons. That observation is from a different and later perspective than my seventeen year old school girl person.

The day of tryouts finally came and it was difficult paying attention in class. I was thinking about what would take place in the gym after school. I could almost hear Miss Myers say, "Why, Betty, I didn't know you could act. You are perfect for the part."

When I walked into the gymnasium, I was surprised to see the number of students lined up to try out for parts. At once I spotted Alicia, a friend from the east end of town. Her parents were French and, for some reason, had wished her to attend public school instead of the parochial school which most of the French children attended. Even so, she had not been truly accepted by the elite west-enders; but then, neither was I. True, I was sometimes on the fringes because of my cousin who was in the center of the west-end social circle. Occasionally, she was required to include me in her activities and the other girls didn't seem to mind.

I asked Alicia which part she intended to try out for and she hesitated a bit, "Well, I was hoping to try out for Meg, but then I decided I'd like to try out for Beth. It is so sad that she has to die, but it would be a great opportunity to do some serious acting. I have always planned to be an actress some day."

Our conversation was interrupted by Miss Myers who reminded us that we must hurry and complete the sign-up sheet indicating the part we wanted to play. Alicia and I soon took care of that little chore and joined the crowd to wait for further instructions. Alicia said, "I have goose bumps just thinking about it. Are you nervous?"

"Yes, a little," I admitted, "but that isn't going to stop me. I feel pretty certain about this. I have a special reason to be positive about getting the part." I didn't share any more with Alicia about praying and asking God to give me the part. She might not understand—not everyone believed in prayer. I was sure she did, though, because she was Catholic and I knew most of them prayed a lot.

The first thing most of us did on arriving at school the next day was to go see the bulletin board just outside the principal's office. Opposite the name *Jo* was Martha Allen. I couldn't believe it. She wasn't right for the part at all. Then I looked down at *Beth* and opposite this was Kathryn Smythe, "Spelled with a 'K,' my dear." She always said so. I forced myself to look at the entire cast of characters. Neither Alicia's nor my name appeared anywhere. I felt devastated. Surely God had let me down.

Later that morning, on the way to English Literature class, I met Alicia. She said, "I want to walk part way home with you today. I'm going in to talk to Miss Myers about those parts. She must have made a mistake somewhere."

I shrugged my shoulders, "It's up to you. I don't want anything to do with the stupid play."

On the way home, Alicia shared with me her conversation with Miss Myers. "She said that both you and I would have been good for the parts, but that she had no choice."

I was shocked at that remark, "No choice? How could that be? She's in charge of the whole production."

Alicia shook her head, "No, she said that she had been told by the principal that she must choose people from the west end because their fathers owned the businesses in town; and they would be contributing financially to the school to buy sets and costumes."

That was my first taste of small-town politics reaching down into my world, and I didn't like it. It just wasn't fair. Besides, I had prayed and I really trusted God to overrule any silly political matters.

I didn't share my feelings with anyone, but disappointment was there, and a bit of anger—mostly at God who had let me down.

When I think back on that early experience I realize I wanted the part for all the wrong reasons and God graciously did not give me what I had asked for. His plan for my life was so much bigger and better than anything I could dream up. It took many years for me to learn to trust him fully but I know without a doubt that my plans aren't always for what I should have. His plan is best.

After World War II broke out and Robby had the 1A classification, soon to be called, he was determined to get into the Air Corps. He told me that he had looked up at the planes and thought how it would be to pilot one. He went to enlist and was told his blood pressure was too high. Come back in a week or so. The same thing happened the next time and they told him not to come back. This was another instance of God's plans being somewhat different from ours. Rob had plans for becoming a hometown hero but God had other plans.

Patriotism was running high in those days. It seemed all the young men wanted to serve their country. My husband was no exception even though he had a wife at home who was pregnant. Robby decided to wait until the draft caught up with him, and that was to be soon. I hated the day that letter from Uncle Sam came in the mail. He was to report the next Tuesday.

I thought *This isn't fair. It's all a dream. No, it's a nightmare! My dreams are beautiful. Robby is God's choice for me. How could He be taking him away from me? Some of my friends' husbands have been killed in battle already. Oh, God, can't you stop it?*

I smiled uncertainly at Robby. He needed me now as much as I needed him. "We will make the most of the time we have left," I said. "I will always pray for you. God will take care of you. Maybe the war won't last long." I spoke with more confidence than I really felt. This war had already lasted longer than most people thought it would.

Robby smiled back. "Yes, we will make every minute count. I'll go to Kansas City to be inducted and then come back for several days before I have to leave for training. At least, that's the way it has been for most of the fellows. For right now, though, we must talk to the folks and arrange for you to move back in with them. I won't have you alone with the baby's birth less than a month away."

I busied myself with packing up the few dishes and other belongings we had in the apartment. Robby's parents said of course they would want me with them when the baby was born. They readied the large room they had for me. It was sweet to find they had placed a newly painted baby crib in there. My heart ached for my husband who knew he couldn't be present to place our newborn infant in it.

We spent the weekend driving around town, talking endlessly about our hopes and dreams for the future. At other times, we just shared each other quietly. We had never experienced such togetherness as we were experiencing now. Neither of us wanted it to end.

Tuesday morning Robby's parents and I took him to the railroad station to leave for Kansas City. He smiled bravely as the train pulled in. "Now don't look so glum. All of you. I will be home tomorrow night and can probably stay for two or three days."

Rob called us that evening. He said, "Guess what? I am in the Navy. I'm catching the first train home but will have to leave on Friday. I'll tell you all about it when I get there." At least he won't be out tramping around in the infantry with enemy soldiers behind every rock. I didn't know much about the logistics of war, but that didn't keep my imagination from running wild. I was suddenly panic stricken. I remembered reading the newspaper headlines relating to the sinking of ships at sea. My heart repeated what it had been saying all along: *I hate this war.*

When Rob came home, he shared with us how he happened to be in the Navy. He said the draftees were placed in a large room and waited for their names to be called. They were then told which branch of the service they would be in. It was commonly said amongst the service men that Uncle Sam just checked to see if you were warm and then told you where to go. Rob had gone to the bathroom and when he returned, one of the fellows said, "Are you Robison? They called your name for the Coast Guard while you were gone. When you didn't answer they took the next fellow. The Coast Guard seemed so desirable that Robby was truly disappointed. About this time they called his name again and, this time, he was placed in the U.S. Navy.

Later on, even the Navy didn't want my precious husband when they found out he was partially color blind. They transferred him to the Navy Seabees where being color blind didn't really matter. He would be a stevedore stationed in Hawaii the entire time. We didn't know anything about where he was stationed because all my mail was strictly censured. I don't think he was allowed to use the word *pineapple* in his letters. He soon learned what was allowed and not many of my letters had strong black marks in them. All of them were stamped **CENSURED** on the outside of the envelopes, however.

When I think about it now, many years later, I am glad Robby was never sent outside Hawaii during the war. Often, the Seabees were sent to other islands to build landing strips before even the Marines were allowed to land. Needless to say, it was dangerous work and many of our brave young men lost their lives serving our country. Rob has complained occasionally, "What kind of stories am I going to tell my grandchildren?" I remind him that he can talk about his later profession as a design engineer building parts for the space shuttle. But it isn't his nature to brag and he doesn't talk much about that.

A verse which is particularly close to my heart now is Jeremiah 29:11, "For I know the plans I have for you," declares the Lord, "plans to prosper you and not to harm you, plans to give you hope and a future..." (NIV) When I shared this verse with Jennifer, it soon became one of her favorites.

CHAPTER TWELVE

Don't be Afraid
God's Promises

After this, the word of the Lord came to Abram in a vision:
Do not be afraid, Abram.
I am your shield, your very great reward.

Genesis 15:1 (NIV)

When Robby was in World War II I kept a picture of him, in his sailor suit, on the dresser. Every night I kissed that picture "goodnight." Denny was a very little boy and didn't know his Daddy except for that picture. I told him that some day his Daddy would come home and we could all be together. But how much can a two or three year old child comprehend? All he knew was that he had a mother and an array of grandparents and aunts and uncles who took pretty good care of him. Meantime, he called every sailor we saw "Daddy."

I am reminded of a verse in the Bible which says that now we see as though looking into an old beat up mirror. The wonderful promise in that same verse is that in the future we will see clearly, face to face, and we will know fully the things we only know partially now. (I Corinthians 13:12)

When we met Rob at the train station upon his release from the Navy, Denny ran straight to him, crying loudly, "Daddy, Daddy." He never called another sailor Daddy after that. He and I had the real thing. We were a complete family now.

Another promise is that we become part of God's family when we believe in His Son, Jesus. Some day, in Heaven, that family, also will become complete.

It is encouraging to know that all our pain and confusion will be wiped away and we will see Christ fully. God has promised us the "real thing." Our future is assured.

Several years ago I was given a little book called *The Bible Promise Book*.

All the promises are scripture verses but grouped under various headings, Anger, Belief, Children, Comfort and many, many others. I don't remember ever having a situation where I looked for a specific heading. However, because I began reading the Bible at a very young age, I have a collection of verses tucked away in my memory bank. Sometimes I find it necessary to look up the exact location in *Strong's Concordance of the Bible*. I hope to draw on some of these verses as I write this chapter. After all, God is "my stronghold and very present help in time of trouble." Now, I know I really should look that up in Strong's but probably won't.

I've mentioned before the anchor verse, John 3:16, which children in almost every Christian home have committed to memory. I often go back to the promise, though, which is contained in this verse. "For God so loved the world, that he gave his only begotten Son, that whosoever believeth in him should not perish, but have everlasting life." (KJV) I am glad I am going to live forever. Not in this body, of course.

Another promise is found in John 1:12. "But as many as received him, to them gave he power to become the sons of God, even to them that believe on his name." I am now a child of God. Last Sunday our pastor said that we are going to live forever as God's "Forever Family." All parents know the importance of the family structure. Some times I feel like a little child. I can't make the right decisions or complete a job as I should. I tell my Heavenly Father about my doubts and He directs and encourages me. It is good to have a family that is going to last forever.

When our children were small, as parents, our every action was to protect and care for them. We wanted them to be happy. They knew of our concern and came to us when things didn't seem to work out right. We encouraged and helped them as much as we could. God wants us to be happy. He has so many plans for our future and our happiness. That leads me to another promise verse I cling to. I spoke of it before but want to mention it again. Jeremiah 29:11 says, "For I know the plans I have for you, declares the Lord, plans to prosper you and not to harm you, plans to give you hope and a future...(NIV).

God has made plans for our future. The grave is not our final destination. We are in the "Forever Family" of God. We really should be anticipating a great family reunion instead of being fearful of every new pain or ailment. I'm looking forward to having a long talk with my friend, and now sister, Jeanette West. She and I both talked about our lack of musical ability here on earth. Neither could carry a tune. She used to say she was going to be singing in God's heavenly choir. I'd like that, too. Perhaps we can stand next to one another. And not a note will be out of place. You can be sure of that.

Because God always answers our earnest prayers, one way or another, Jeanette is singing lustily in that heavenly choir. She had asked God, the Father, to give her a servant's heart and He did it in a most spectacular way. Now she is able to sing with the best of them.

I once had a little taste of what it will be like. I was a counselor at a Billy Graham Crusade. We arrived a little late and there were no seats left. An usher told me that he had a vacant seat in the choir. The soprano section, no less. I hesitated and he said, "Don't let it bother you. Just mouth the words." I did that and was surrounded by all those wonderful voices. It was heavenly.

Another verse which is very dear to me is Matthew 6:6. It reads, "But thou, when thou prayest, enter into thy closet, and when thou hast shut the door, pray to thy Father which is in secret; and thy Father which seeth in secret shall reward thee openly."

In the Fall, when our church had its annual revival meeting, I had been experiencing a great deal of discomfort and unrest in my soul. I was a girl of fifteen and faithfully attended church but wasn't getting much out of it. At the meeting, I allowed my mind to wander and didn't hear all the evangelist said. Now and then, I was brought back to the present when he shouted and pounded vigorously on the pulpit. I had missed his preceding remarks and, of course, missed the point. I wondered if that old pulpit could take all that pounding.

At the conclusion of the meeting there was an *altar call* as the congregation sang. I arbitrarily rejected much of what was being said, but when the altar call was given, I was drawn to go forward with several others and knelt at the altar rail. I felt overcome with guilt and confusion. Well-meaning women advised me to "pray through." First, I was instructed that I must "lay all on the altar." The phrase was explained—give up lipstick, nail polish, jewelry, short skirts, (that meant "anything above the ankles"), even marriage if God so decreed. My stubborn soul refused. So much to give up. The issue was so clouded with negativism that I went home feeling miserable.

The next day I could bear the misery no longer. I was determined not to go back to that altar of my confusion, but knew I must have peace of mind. In my Bible I had read that when you pray you should go into your closet alone. In our upstairs bedroom in the old farmhouse there was a very large closet. I went in and closed the door. I fell to my knees and wept. I didn't know the right words, but I was sure they had nothing to do with lipstick and nail polish. I admitted my wretched condition and asked God to give me peace. It may not have been the prescribed prayer for sinners, but God accepted it and I know He accepted me!

As I opened the door of my heart to Him, Christ Jesus walked in and the floodgates of heaven opened simultaneously. The closet and my bedroom seemed flooded with light. My vocabulary had a new word and I could say only "Glory, Glory, Glory!" I sensed that the angels in heaven were singing and rejoicing with me. I was a new baby born into God's wonderful family! True, I had been willful and had wanted no part of the "midwives" at the church altar, but God so graciously allowed me to be born anyway. I resolved that, from that day on, I would rely on the Bible for knowing God and not worry about fitting into any of the molds of men.

The uneasy guilty feeling I'd had for so long was gone. I realized how much I loved everyone around me, even the ladies with long hair in buns and faces to match. Surely they ought to know that God isn't negative but, oh, so very positive.

The God-imposed disciplines necessary for spiritual growth I was to learn later. For now, I was a happy child completely at peace with myself because I was at peace with God. What I had done was, in essence, what those ladies had wanted me to do. I had submitted to God and asked Him to control my life. We have a patient, loving and totally awesome God!

My Grandmother Lewis gave me some great advice before I was married. I had told her how special Robby was and how eager we were to be married. She said, "Well, it will work if you always remember not to let the sun go down on your anger. Get your arguments settled before you go to sleep."

I learned she was using Ephesians 4:26 which says "Be ye angry and sin not: let not the sun go down upon your wrath." KJV of course. Over the years I have practiced that advice many times. Wonderful as my husband is, we sometimes disagree. I try never to go to sleep angry. I think there is a promise from God in that verse. It is possible, with God's help to be angry and not sin. There is also a command for us. Don't let the anger fester. Never go to sleep angry. God's promises sometimes are accompanied by a command or instruction to follow. We should look for both, of course. God cares about our concerns. Turning every situation over to Him has helped me many times.

When we asked Mother to live with us she was already 80 years of age and quite set in some of her ways. Both Robby and I were retirement age and had anticipated doing lots of traveling when Rob did retire. We changed our plans somewhat with another person to be responsible for. We were able to do some traveling but always felt it necessary to arrange to have someone stay with Mother. At times I became impatient with my mother and I'm sure she with me. I resorted to a Bible promise often. "Honour thy father and mother; (which is the first commandment with promise;) that it may be well with thee, and thou mayest live long on the earth." Ephesians 6:1-3. (KJV)

At the time, I wasn't convinced that I wanted to live long on the earth. I find now that the older I get the less eager I am to leave this earth. I am certain, though, that Mother and I will have lots to talk about when I see her in Heaven. We certainly will not disagree with one another or become impatient as we did on earth. I'm glad to know those things were temporary. Eternity will be different.

Mother had been with us for ten years when she began to tire of living, I think. She was ninety years of age and becoming, we thought, more childish every day. One morning I went into her bedroom to ask what she would like for breakfast. She was curled up in bed in a fetal position.

"Mother, what is wrong? Where do you hurt?"

She answered, "All over."

She didn't want anything to eat and refused to get out of bed. We had been to see her doctor the week before and he assured us she was in excellent health for her age. There was no need for any additional medication. I felt totally helpless and a little irritated. With her, with myself, with God. Why didn't He do something?

As I walked out of the room, the phone was ringing. I answered and was glad to hear my sister, Dorothy's voice. She and her husband, Leonard lived in our home town of Concordia, Kansas. She immediately asked me what was wrong. I explained to her my frustration.

"It's Mother. I think she has given up. My nerves are a mess. She won't get out of bed or eat anything. Yet she says she is still flying to Kansas for "Decoration" Day. How could she do that?"

Every year Mother enjoyed flying back to Kansas for a two or three week stay with Dorothy and Leonard. The airline people put her in a wheel chair and treated her like royalty. In the Midwest the folks make much more of Memorial Day than we do on the West Coast. They place flowers on all the graves and have ceremonies at the cemetery especially honoring the fallen service men. My father and my brother, Harold, had been in the service of our country. Daddy and Harold are buried in the Concordia cemetery and Mother made plans to be "laid away" there.

Dorothy seemed to understand my predicament. She said, "I think Mother will improve enough to fly back here in a week or so. I also think you have been responsible for Mother long enough. It is time Leonard and I took over."

I was relieved, and at the same time, filled with guilt. As a Christian I was certain I should have been able to cope with any situation. After all, isn't that what God's promises are all about? I have since come to understand that God has made all of us with certain physical limitations. I had reached mine and couldn't admit it.

We talked with Mother and she assured us she felt perfectly well enough to fly to Kansas. Just thinking about it seemed to give her the stamina she needed. When she arrived in Kansas, Dorothy called and said Mother was quite chipper and was apparently enjoying the visit.

Even though we had bought a round trip ticket for Mother, Dorothy and Leonard were able to convince her that she should stay indefinitely with them. For two years Robby and I were able to begin the travel we had planned much earlier. That is when we joined the volunteer organization, MMAP. The organization sent us on three week work assignments to various church camps, Indian reservations, rescue missions, and other Christian projects. We now had our opportunity to travel with a purpose. Every MMAP family was required to have a self-contained RV and travel anywhere in the United States that we were sent. I think there were even some projects in Alaska. We didn't choose to do one of those.

In September, before Mother's ninety-third birthday, Dorothy called to tell us that Mother had died of an aortic aneurysm the night before. With Judy and Andy, we drove to Kansas for the funeral. After we came home I began to be filled with guilt. Why hadn't I relied on the Lord to keep her with us until she died? I think that is what she wanted. Is it necessary to be so weak as I was?

One day when I was lashing myself with all those guilt questions, I dropped to my knees and cried, "Lord, she died before I had a chance to show her how much I loved her." One thing I know, we have a loving Father. He spoke to my heart with words as clear as if they had been audible, "She knows. She knows." God has promised us His peace and He certainly provided it that day.

I spoke before about Rainbow Acres, the ranch for mentally handicapped adults. They can dress and feed themselves and do very simple chores, but like most children they do not have mature judgment. They live with "house parents." We became acquainted with most of them and they treated us like family.

The ranch, Rainbow Acres, invited us to an open house and program they were having on a grassy hillside. We put blankets on the ground and enjoyed the program immensely. I was still grieving for the loss of my mother. I told that to a house parent friend nearby. I hadn't noticed Tommy, a Downs Syndrome "boy" on the same blanket.

Downs Syndrome people are usually very loving and compassionate. Tommy overheard my conversation. He said, "Your Mama died? My Mama died too." Then Tommy reached over and patted me on the shoulder. What an act of love. I wanted to hug Tommy but he is not comfortable with hugs. The pat on the shoulder was as much reaching out as he could manage. God's comfort comes in many forms.

Not one of all the Lord's good promises to the house of Israel failed; every one was fulfilled.

Joshua 21:45 (NIV)

CHAPTER THIRTEEN

Being Conformed to Christ's Image

*For those whom He foreknew, He also predestined to be
conformed to the image of His Son, in order that He might
be the first-born among many brethren.*

Romans 8:29 (RSV)

I remember seeing a television commercial in which a
child, no more than a toddler was walking down a path
with his father. The boy obviously was trying to follow in his
daddy's footsteps, walking like his dad, and imitating everything his father did. It was endearing because most of us can
relate to the scene. We so often see children imitating the one
they love.

I thought how we Christians, when no more than toddlers
in our faith, truly want to imitate Jesus Christ. The key here
is that we must want to be like Christ. We have already taken
that first step of faith by accepting what Christ has done for
us and becoming "born again" believers. Jesus Christ, God's
Son, existed before his birth on earth. That Christ would be
born as a human baby was part of God's great plan for our

salvation. Thus, even after being born physically as babies, God intends that we have the experience of being "born again." That is how we become part of God's large family.

God knew those who would take that first step and planned that each one of us would become like His "Perfect Son." Sometimes I puzzle over the part I am to play in "being conformed to Christ." I know that I first must want to be like Jesus. Then begins the process. Rick Warren, in his book *The Purpose Driven Life* says, "Christlikeness is your destination, but your journey will last a lifetime."

Galatians 2:20 explains this truth more fully. "I have been crucified with Christ; it is no longer I who live, but Christ lives in me; and the life which I now live in the flesh I live by faith in the Son of God, who loved me and gave Himself for me." Some scriptures are a whole bundle of truths and I think this is one of those.

Last week I asked our pastor if he had any helpful material on "being conformed to Christ's image." He mentioned several authors who addressed this issue, Ian Thomas, Watchman Nee, and others. As I looked over my books, I found several others and am finding them helpful in learning how better to become conformed to Christ's image.

Also, the pastor suggested I go on the internet and have Google do a search on Galatians 2:20. I did that and discovered that they had printed the first ten of about 250,000. Well, well, there must be a great deal of interest in the subject, especially in the Christian world.

One of the books on my shelves is *In His Steps* by Charles M. Sheldon. This little book is a classic. In the Foreward of the book I read that Dr. Sheldon had written this book in the month of July, 1896, to be used in an attempt to create interest in the Sunday night preaching service of his church in Topeka, Kansas. He said he wrote the book outside sitting on his porch when temperatures went up to 104 degrees.

I remember well those sweltering summer days and nights in Kansas. As a child growing up I may not have noticed the heat as much as the adults. I do remember that Mother let us children sleep on the floor anywhere in the house which seemed to be coolest. We liked the informality of throwing a blanket and pillow on the floor and talking to our siblings into the wee hours of the morning.

But back to the book, I have read that only a few copies of the book were published at first. The whole premise of *In His Steps* was that each of us should commit ourselves to ask one simple question before making any decision. "What would Jesus do?" When a Christian takes the time to study God's word and become acquainted with Jesus in a personal way, asking that question causes us to weigh our actions. The characters in the book experienced changed lives and lifestyles within the year of their commitment.

As I said, the book has become a classic in Christian circles. I remember not too long ago while in the hospital I saw a nurse with a ribbon around her neck which had the initials WWJD on it. The idea has spread widely and many of us are now trying to be like Jesus. That is, after all, God's plan for every believer. We are to be conformed to the image of Jesus Christ. By the way, Sheldon's book has sold millions of copies in America, Canada, and England. I don't know how many other countries have published it.

An even older classic that I have on the shelf is *The Imitation of Christ* by Thomas a. Kempis. This man wrote from an Augustine convent near Zwolle in the Netherlands in the 1400's. He made a comment on John 14:6, "I am the way, the truth, and the life. Without the way, there is no going; without the truth, there is no knowing; without the life, there is no living." For five hundred years this little classic has been helping Christian believers understand better how to imitate Christ.

Another book I find helpful is *The Saving Life of Christ,* written by Ian Thomas, the British Major who has had a very productive ministry in England and the United States. In the explanatory section of this book we read " Major Thomas points out how many dedicated people, ministers, Sunday School teachers, and the like, have come out of the old life but never gone on to the full, joyous life in Christ. He writes with fresh insight into many Bible passages, and challenges Christians to walk on and take the victory that is already won." The fullness of life which God expects of all believers is that we become like His Son, Jesus Christ.

I am convinced now in the winter of my life on earth that conforming us to Christ's image is just the Holy Spirit working to tie up the loose ends before we go on to the next segment of our lives, which is meeting Christ in Heaven.

We have hanging on the wall of our home a little plaque which gives the "Fruit of the Spirit." The Holy Spirit works in each of us to make us like Christ and I believe the work He is doing is also developing that fruit in every believer Someone has said that the fruit epitomizes the character of Christ. I think as I finish this chapter I will examine each of those items and try to see how nearly they may match my character.

"But the fruit of the Spirit is love, joy, peace, patience, kindness, goodness, faithfulness, gentleness and self-control." Galatians 5:22-25 (NIV)

Love. I remember well when I was asked to go to Northern California to be trained by Miss Johnson to become a Bible Study Fellowship Teaching Leader. I was frightened at the prospect of standing before a large auditorium of women. The Fullerton class had an enrollment of 450 women with a waiting list of 100. I had often used the verse from II Timothy. *For God hath not given us the spirit of fear; but of power, and of love, and of a sound mind.* Being a very timid and fearful person once, when the children were small and

I was ill, I had lain awake for hours at night worrying about dying before the children were grown. I prayed, "Oh, God, you know that Robby would get married again and I don't think anyone would understand our children as I do. I'm so afraid." Out of the dark I heard, not audibly, "God didn't give you a spirit of fear." The next day I looked up the passage and from then on leaned heavily on that promise. Nothing should make me fearful. And, of course, some things did, but I always clung to that verse. I told myself *My fear does not come from God, so I must abandon it.* That usually worked and I became a confident Christian again.

Now, I was being prepared for a task I was certain I could not do. I began quoting the passage from II Timothy. I prayed *Please, God, give me the power to stand before all those ladies and teach your word in a meaningful way. I need power, your power. That is a lot of ladies, Lord. Large bunches of people scare me.*

Again, God spoke to my heart. **Just love them.** For several days I was rather puzzled by God's answer. Of course, I loved them. I thought I loved everyone. I was soon to learn that there is great strength and power in love. Also, we can't do it alone. There were many times I had to ask God to love through me. Some folks can be mighty hard to love. But God loves even the unlovely. I learned to do it, too.

Joy. The next of Christ's characteristics to examine is Joy. Sometimes I didn't feel full of joy. Today, for instance, I am more cranky than joyful. I complain, "My back hurts, I'm tired." Then, I need to go back to Nave's Topical Bible and re-examine all the passages on Joy. Often, I become a little child and by rote say "The joy of the Lord is my strength." I'm finding that all of the fruit of the spirit comes from God. So where I am weak, He is strong. Didn't Paul say something like that?

Peace. A melody has been going through my head. I can't remember all the words of the familiar hymn but I remember the first line, *When peace, like a river, attendeth my way...*In an old hymn book I found the song, *It is Well With My Soul.* That's it! I looked on my bookshelves for a book I remember having that gives the background story of a number of hymns. It seems to be missing. I probably gave it away. Try the Google search again. There has to be some information on the internet. There is. A very sad story from most folks' standpoint. "The hymn was written after two major traumas in Horatio Spafford's life. The first was the great Chicago Fire of October 1871, which ruined him financially (he had been a wealthy businessman). Shortly after, while crossing the Atlantic, all four of Spafford's daughters died in a collision with another ship. Spafford's wife, Anna, survived and sent him the now famous telegram, 'Saved alone.' Several weeks later, as Spafford's own ship passed near the spot where his daughters died, the Holy Spirit inspired these words. They speak to the eternal hope that all believers have, no matter what pain and grief befall them on earth."

The music was composed by Philip P. Bliss, 1876. The tune is named after the ship on which Spafford's children perished, the *S.S. Ville de Havre.* Ironically, Bliss himself died in a tragic train wreck shortly after writing this music.

And we think we have troubles! However, this story does clearly show the great extent of God's love and the peace He can give His followers.

The words are worth considering:

When peace, like a river, attendeth my way,
When sorrows like sea billows roll;
Whatever my lot, Thou has taught me to say
It is well, it is well, with my soul.

Though Satan should buffet, though trials should
  come
Let this blest assurance control,

That Christ has regarded my helpless estate,
And hath shed His own blood for my soul.

My sin, oh, the bliss of this glorious thought!
My sin, not in part but the whole,
Is nailed to the cross, and I bear it no more,
Praise the Lord, praise the Lord, O my soul!

For me, be it Christ, be it Christ hence to live:
If Jordan above me shall roll,
No pang shall be mine, for in death as in life
Thou wilt whisper "Thy peace to my soul."

But, Lord, 'tis for Thee, for Thy coming we wait,
The sky, not the grave, is our goal;
Oh trump of the angel! Oh voice of the Lord!
Blessed hope, blessed rest of my soul!

And Lord, haste the day when my faith shall
    be sight,
The clouds be rolled back as a scroll;
The trump shall resound, and the Lord shall
    descend,
Even so, it is well with my soul.

The peace this man, Spafford, experienced is similar to how I felt after praying in that farmhouse closet so many years ago, "Lord, please give me peace." It is what Robby and I pray for daily for our grandchildren and great grandchildren who may not know the Lord yet.

Yesterday we attended a memorial service for a very dear friend who has now discovered what the words of this song really mean. Our friend, Doris, a wonderful Christian lady, had been vibrant and well six months ago. After being diagnosed with brain cancer her body deteriorated quickly and, within three months, she was with the Lord in Heaven. Yesterday we saw her husband, Bob, with a tranquil, peaceful expression on his face. He said he was thankful they had that three months to reminisce, talk and just rest in the Lord.

Patience. Because I tend to associate patience with learning to curb one's temper, I thought it best to check with Webster. The dictionary explanation is: "patience, n. 1. The bearing of provocation, annoyance, misfortune or pain without complaint, loss of temper, or anger. 2. An ability or willingness to suppress restlessness or annoyance when confronted with delay. 3. Quiet, steady perseverance; even-tempered care, diligence."

There does seem to be more involved here than just "don't lose your temper." As a child I had a quick temper. I remember at a very early age hearing some of my aunts or uncles say, "She's just like her dad. Can't control her temper." Many years later, when I became interested in living for the Lord, I prayed, "Lord, please take away my temper." I think He has done that very thing. Oh, I still flare up if I see a child or animal being mistreated. The difference now is that I pray and ask God to take care of the injustice. I have grown up a bit spiritually. That is part of the Holy Spirit conforming each of us to Christ's image.

However, according to Webster, *patience* has more to do with other facets of my character than my temper. Consider experiencing misfortune or pain without annoyance or complaint. I might try to "grin and bear it" but there is always a little annoyance. Also, I can't suppress restlessness or annoyance when confronted with delay.

How many times have we been in a line of traffic and are held up so long the ice cream we bought at the store has begun to melt? Now, that makes me annoyed! I am convinced that the Holy Spirit still has much to do in my life teaching me to be patient as Christ was patient.

Kindness. I am told this refers to a person who is considerate and compassionate. There are people I've met who are considerate and compassionate but who do not profess to be believers in Jesus Christ. Nevertheless, God tells us in His Word that He wants us to be kind. In Philippians 2:3 we are told "Do nothing out of selfish ambition or vain conceit, but in humility consider others better than yourselves." Paul goes on to explain that even Christ thought of others first and we should have the same attitude. With that attitude, kindness is bound to follow.

Goodness. A fruit of the Spirit. As with kindness, also a fruit of the Spirit, sometimes an unbeliever can be a very good person. And, as with kindness, if the Holy Spirit is to conform us to Christ's image, we must be "good." Christ, Himself, was undeniably a good person. I want to be like Him.

Faithfulness. Proverbs 20:6 says a faithful man is hard to find. Yet, in my experience, there have been many faithful persons, as well as unfaithful persons. A faithful person is a dependable person.

One of the things I love about my husband is that I can always depend on him. If he says he will be somewhere, he's there. Over the years others have noticed and commented on how dependable he is. He told me the other day that his father was also that kind of man. So Robby had a good role model when he was growing up.

I recall that when we went to Scotland we looked up the Robison tartan and crest. We bought each of our boys the crest and I find it interesting that above the name Robison has been inscribed "Faithful." What a legacy to live up to. But it is nothing in comparison to how faithful Jesus, our Savior, is. May every one of us hear the Lord say to us in Heaven, "Well done, thou good and faithful servant."

Gentleness. Not long ago we were able to get in touch with a friend from our past. She is a widow now. She and her husband were friends of ours when our children and theirs were very young. She wrote me that hearing from us was so refreshing and that she had talked with her younger sister who, in years past, worked with Robby at the aircraft company. She said her sister remembered Robby as being a very gentle man, actually a true gentleman.

I wonder what it takes in our lives for the Holy Spirit to be able to develop gentleness? Some people are just naturally more gentle than others. Some are rough around the edges by nature. But for every believer, God wants us to be conformed to Christ's image. Christ, while firm, was gentle at all times. I'll have to pray about that for myself.

Self-control. Why does God include "self-control" and not "Christ-controlled" in the fruit of the Spirit? I believe it is because every one of us has to make a conscious choice to become a Christian. That is one way God has made every human being in His image. We are free to make our own choices, good or bad. The Holy Spirit, Himself, helps us to make the right choices. If we choose to believe what Christ has done for us on the cross then we can become a child of God. We then enter into the family relationship and belong for eternity.

Jesus said that He chose to lay down His life for us. No one took it from Him. To become a believer we must accept what He did so willingly for us. I truly want to be like Him.

CHAPTER FOURTEEN

Heaven

The Lord is in His holy temple, the Lord's throne is in heaven.

Psalm 11:4

I have really enjoyed reading and re-reading the books I have on heaven. I think one of the most fascinating is a book called *Heaven* by Randy Alcorn. In this book we are introduced to a new way of looking at heaven. For so many years I have puzzled over the question of whether or not we receive new bodies when we die. I know we are promised new bodies but it would seem that we can't receive them until Christ returns to earth a second time. Will we be disembodied spirits when we go to live with Jesus? I think part of my discomfort with facing death has been that I do not like the idea of being only a spirit. It is so beyond my imagination. The author tells us that God made us to be comfortable in physical bodies surrounded by familiar things and places.

Randy Alcorn suggests that when we die we go to an intermediate heaven. He says it is a physical place and we will probably have physical bodies, perfect but physical. He believes, and I am beginning to see the reasoning, that God has prepared this intermediate place for us until a time when He will take us to live with Him on the new earth.

We will have new bodies, glorified, but awaiting the resurrection. Human beings are both spiritual and physical. We are more at home with the physical usually because that is what we are most familiar with. It is well to remember that God created Adam's body first and then breathed into it a spirit. (Genesis 2:7)

I am comfortable with most of Alcorn's premises but find that there is one premise I need to think about. He feels, as I do, that God has created an actual material place called "Heaven." We know that Christ, after His resurrection, came back for a period of time and then ascended to Heaven. The book of Acts tells us that. Jesus, at that time, though He had a glorified body, actually had a physical body. He wore clothing and ascended fully dressed. The book, *Heaven,* offers the explanation that because Christ, with a physical body and dressed in a material way ascended to Heaven, that place is inhabited by at least one physical Person, fully dressed. Mr. Alcorn feels it is very likely that we will wear clothing in both the intermediate heaven and our final heavenly home.

He may be right but I can't help exploring the fact that Adam and Eve lived in a perfect environment before they sinned. They did not wear any clothing nor feel any shame until they had sinned. Then, of course, we know the story tells us they made coverings for themselves of fig leaves. God did not accept their vain attempt to cover up their sin. Being naked was not the sin. Disobedience to God was. Scripture plainly tells us that we will live forever in a renewed heaven and earth. Not new, but renewed to their former perfect state.

I don't know if we would be more comfortable with clothing or not. I truly believe that heaven, whether the intermediate one or the final one, will be a perfect place for us to live forever. There are some things I can't solve with my finite mind but I know that I have a loving Father in heaven who wants the best for me.

I wrote a book once for a friend who had lost both her husband and her 10 year old son in tragic accidents. She said, "I agonized over not knowing if my husband had accepted the Lord and would be spending eternity with me. A pastor friend assured me that God had my best interests at heart and He knew the answer to my question. I might not know until I got to heaven. Suddenly, I was at peace. My loving heavenly Father God knew and that was enough."

I don't have to have all the answers while on this earth. God has given me the information He wants me to have. In addition, I seem to be learning something new from His word every day. I just need to have my heart tuned to His instruction and guidance. He loves me and I am learning to love Him more each day.

Several years ago my sister, Charlotte, and husband, Alan, lived in Las Vegas, Nevada. He was a Gerber baby food salesman and when Charlotte heard their company was moving them to Las Vegas she said, "Oh no, we're moving to Sodom and Gomorrah!" Actually, they became active in a local church and things worked out fine for them. While they were there Charlotte obtained a small teacup poodle and had it bred. She asked me if I would take one of the puppies. We had not had a dog for some time and were a bit reluctant but I finally agreed. Claudia was taking French in High School and volunteered to name the tiny registered French poodle. We found it would need three names and she christened our little one *Nicole Claudette Simone*. We thought it was a very fancy name but agreed to call her Nicky.

We obtained another small French Poodle and named him *Mr. French*. He was to be Nicky's husband. Sure enough Nicky became pregnant and the veterinarian told us Nicky was too small to deliver her babies normally. She had a caesarian section and delivered two tiny babies. They were immediately placed in oxygen and one died in the night. The other survived and we were proud owners of another teacup poodle. We eventually gave both that dog and Mr. French to friends and had Nicky spayed. No more babies for her. She was too small to begin with.

Nicky lived for about fifteen years and developed a heart condition. She was on heart medication for one year. By that time both of the girls were married. I was teaching Bible Study Fellowship and Mother was living with us. She attended the Bible class with me. That kept me on my toes. If I said something she didn't agree with she set me straight.

One morning I was getting ready to go to class. Nicky sat at my feet whining. I picked her up and put her on a small pillow on the counter. She looked up at me but didn't stir. She was definitely a lap dog. Once, she whined and I picked her up and held her close. She laid her head on my arm, looked up at me and then with a sigh dropped her head. I knew something was wrong.

I was torn. Four hundred women were waiting at the church to hear me proclaim the gospel. A little dog I loved needed help. I took her to the car, laid her on the pillow and drove to our nearby veterinary hospital. I walked in and said, "Nicky is in the car. I think she is in a coma." The nurse walked out with me and examined Nicky, "No, she's gone. We can take care of it."

I drove back home and explained to Mother what had happened. I said, "Mother, I must teach that class. Nicky is dead. Now, don't tell anyone at class what has happened. Just pray for me."

Mother usually rode to class with our next door neighbor so I could go early. She did so that day. I prayed all the way to the church *Lord you know I loved that little dog. But she was just a dog and all those ladies with eternal souls that need to be reached are waiting. Help me please to present the gospel clearly this morning. Amen.*

Of course Mother did tell one friend, Gerri Shaw. Gerri didn't see how I could have gone on with my lecture as though nothing had happened. Gerri was a new Christian and also a dog lover. I had told her that I did not think our pets go to heaven because Christ died on the cross for human beings who have souls and can make commitments to live for Christ.

Gerri studied scripture most of her waking hours. She told me once, "I just know that dogs go to heaven. I'll find it in the Bible and show you." She never did and now she is in heaven with the Lord.

The reason I wanted to tell about the incident is that, many years later, as I am reading Randy Alcorn's book on heaven, I see he has a chapter entitled "Will Animals, Including our Pets, Live Again?" There are some very thought-provoking statements in this chapter. Alcorn quoted John Wesley "If the Creator and Father of every living thing is rich in mercy towards all…how is it that misery of all kinds overspreads the face of the earth? …All the beasts of the field, and all the fowls of the air, were with Adam in paradise. And there is no question but their state was suited to their place: It was paradisiacal; perfectly happy."

Alcorn also quotes Joni Eareckson Tada who wrote in her book about Heaven, "If God brings our pets back to life, it wouldn't surprise me. It would be just like Him. It would be totally in keeping with His generous character…"

I don't know but it is possible I may have to admit to Gerri when I get to heaven that I made a mistake when I told her that pets don't go to heaven. She may have one of her favorite pets of the past sitting at her heels. If pets are there it won't be because they accepted what Christ did on the cross for them. It will be because God who loves His children so much has given those pets back to their original owners to add to their joy in heaven. God certainly knows how to give good gifts to each of us both now and in the future.

Another little book I have enjoyed is *Heaven, My Father's Home* by Anne Graham Lotz, Billy Graham's daughter. She tells of driving up to the mountain home of her mother and father and being admitted through the gate because she is her father's daughter. She tells us that is how it will be when we enter heaven. Our entrance is assured if we belong to the family of God. The Bible tells us how to become a child of God. We must accept what His Son, Jesus Christ, has done for us by dying on the cross and paying the penalty for our sins.

When we moved to Arizona we looked for a suitable lot to build a home. In California we had become used to living in rather large two story homes. Now, with just the two of us it was time to scale down to something smaller. We found a lot and builder and arranged to have a one story home built. A three bedroom home was just what we thought we needed. There was a front and back yard for our two small dogs to play in. On our fiftieth wedding anniversary Robby put up a white picket fence in the front for me. I had always wanted one. We planned to stay in that location for the rest of our lives. However, fifteen years later both of us had health problems which made it necessary to look for an even smaller home without the yard work. We bought and moved into the townhome where we live now.

I have missed having a yard and rather enviously look at the individual homes for sale in this same development. On the street next to ours we saw a home that was for sale. To me it was perfect. I began calling it "my home." The front and back yards had been landscaped beautifully and I often dreamed of selling our home and buying that one. Of course, the dream was not a practical one. We had moved so that Robby would not have to trim trees, plant shrubs, and climb on the roof to clean gutters or check the air conditioner. But I am a dreamer and was so disappointed when someone else bought that house. Robby reminded me, "God has a home in heaven for us that is far larger and finer than that one." He was right, of course.

Alcorn suggests there will be physical homes with streets and all the things we enjoy most like trees, flowers and shrubs about. That sounds so inviting. A perfect place to be in perfect bodies with sin abolished. In other words, a perfect world.

Alcorn quotes A. W. Tozer, one of my favorite writers, "The church is constantly being tempted to accept this world as her home . . . but if she is wise she will consider that she stands in the valley between the mountain peaks of eternity past and eternity to come. The past is gone forever and the present is passing as swift as the shadow on the sundial of Ahaz. Even if the earth should continue a million years not one of us could stay to enjoy it. We do well to think of the long tomorrow."

There is a poem by Martha Snell Nicholson, from the book *Ivory Palaces,* which has always helped me get a better perspective on Eternity.

ETERNITY

I stood with God on the edge of the world, and my hand was in His hand. I looked down the road of the past, as it stretched away in the dim distance, 'til it was shrouded in the mists of time. And I knew it had no beginning, and a little chill wind of fear blew about my head:

God asked, "Are you afraid?"

And I said, "Yes, because I cannot understand how there can be no beginning."

So God said, "Let us turn and face the other way."

And I looked into glory, and my heart rejoiced with joy
unspeakable, and then my mind went ahead, a billion,
billion years, and I knew there would be no end, and again
that little chill wind of fear began to blow.

And God asked me again, "Are you afraid?"

And I answered, "A little, because I cannot understand how
there can be no end."

So God asked me tenderly, "Are you afraid now, today,
with your hand in mine?"

And I looked up at Him and smiled and replied,
"Oh, my Father, No!"

And God said, "Every day in eternity will be today."

Robby and I meet twice a month with a small group
of folks, seven in all, to study scripture and pray for one
another. We have wonderful fellowship and have become so
well acquainted with one another that we know we can safely
confide any of our cares or concerns. That small group, I
believe, represents what heaven will be like. People caring
for others as God cares for all of us.

Several years ago our son, Jerry, and his wife Jenny
were divorced. Ever since, Jerry has called us faithfully
each Sunday evening. I usually answer the phone because
Robby does not hear well. Jerry has grown as a Christian in
so many ways. We are able to talk about what the pastor said
that morning, what certain passages of scripture mean and,
often, just what is on our hearts at the moment. To me, it is
a very precious time and I believe Jerry also enjoys it. He
never seems to be in a hurry to get to other things. Both of

us agreed this week to pray more for Jenny. She needs God's reassurance in her life at this time.

I mention the two events above because I believe they give us a glimpse of what heaven will be like. Both A. W. Tozer and Martha Snell Nicholson are with the Lord and we may be able to have extended conversations with each of them.

At one time, when we were traveling with MMAP we bought a new Bounder motorhome. Chris and Tina were small and came over to our house to see the new R.V. Tina Oh-h-ed and Ah-h-ed and then said, "Grampa, we know what these things cost. You must be spending our inheritance."

We all got a laugh out of that. But I pray that Tina will discover that her real inheritance is not on this earth. Anne Graham Lotz wrote "Heaven is the inheritance of God's children."

CHAPTER FIFTEEN

Home at Last

*In my Father's house are many mansions; if it were not so,
I would have told you.
I go to prepare a place for you.*

John 14:2 (KJV)

I was asked to be an Advisor for a Billy Graham Crusade in the Coliseum in Los Angeles and was glad to be used for Christ that way. We were instructed to follow up the Counselors and make certain the inquirer knew he or she was a Christian. I would be working with the children. All of us were kept busy at that crowded overflow meeting. I walked up to one little boy, eight or ten years of age. I asked him why he had come forward. He shrugged his shoulders and said, "Well, I wanted to see what Billy Graham looked like up close."

That particular evening all of us had been warned that Mr. Graham's life had been threatened but the meeting would go on as planned. It did and, so far as we know, nothing unusual happened. The little boy I talked with, of course, was just an innocent child who was also very honest. I talked with him and prayed with him and do not know any more about him.

I began thinking how difficult it is to get near the famous and well known folks of our world. In heaven we won't even have to make an appointment. All of us will be equal and have an eternity to talk things over. Even God our heavenly Father and Jesus Christ will be nearby. As God restores heaven and earth to its original state, we can walk and talk with our Lord just as Adam and Eve did before they sinned.

Billy Graham and I are about the same age and I don't know which of us will get to heaven first. It can't be many years for either of us, of course. Anyway, I think that I shall look up God's evangelist and talk awhile. I'll ask him how he managed to be so calm that night when his life had been threatened. "I didn't really do it, Betty. God did. Others were concerned but I told them that God was totally in control. He wanted to get his message out to many people and He did. I didn't do anything but proclaim the message."

"You know, Billy, I understand in a small way what you are saying. God entrusted me with His message also. Not to large stadiums but to hundreds of women. Bible Study Fellowship was one of the instruments He used at that time. I met your daughter, Anne, at a teaching leader's seminar. She and I happened to be sitting at the same table for lunch. I knew she was a young mother at that time, about the age of our Claudia. Claudia, herself, was being used as a discussion leader in Bible Study Fellowship. Anne and I discussed how difficult it was sometimes to juggle all the duties of a mother and a Bible teacher. And now just look at how far Anne has come as a writer and teacher of the Bible. And Claudia is so faithful as a chaplain in a general hospital."

"Yes, God was good to us, Betty, to give us children who would serve Him faithfully. Ruth and I are very grateful. What a wonderful Savior and Father we have!"

It is exciting to know we can have long visits with other believers and worshippers when we get to Heaven! And we won't need to make an appointment no matter how famous they may have been on earth. I think I may want to talk a few things over with Paul and maybe with Abraham. I've studied Genesis many times and there are a few questions that still haven't been answered. I believe I will ask Abraham what influenced him to believe there was a God in heaven entirely different from the pagan gods the folks in Ur of the Chaldeans worshipped. Somehow the same God I know and love made Himself known to Abraham. How did He do that?

Because time is not an issue in heaven, I shall discuss and question at length every Bible hero I've read about. Then I might begin having conversations with my loved ones who have preceded me in death.

I don't feel I ever really knew my mother. One picture I have of her was taken when she was twenty or twenty-one. She had the loveliest hands in that picture. And, of course, her large brown eyes added to her beauty. I didn't see her in later years as a physically beautiful person. I saw her as a crotchety old lady, at times just as I am today. But she once was young and beautiful. She had plans and dreams I'm sure. I'd like to ask her about her childhood. She once told me that she had been somewhat of a tomboy. She said that all the little girls wore long dresses. Hers often got in her way and she would pin the skirt up between her legs for makeshift pants so she could climb over fences.

"Mother" I'll ask "Tell me about when you first saw Daddy. Did you fall in love then or did he keep coming around until you began to think about marrying him?"

"He actually came around to see my brothers. They were all interested in motorcycles. One day he noticed me. I had on a pretty dress and it was not pinned up, I'm sure. But he asked me to ride his motorcycle. I told him I didn't think so but would go with him when he bought a car. Those old cars weren't much then. We had been riding in buggies with horses. Your daddy was working and I knew he could buy a car. He had been to war and had a little money anyway. So he bought a Model T Ford and we went riding right into marriage." She smiled and I knew she was the most beautiful woman I had ever seen.

I wondered how my grandmother Lewis managed to cope with her tomboy daughter. So I sat down on a curb and asked her about my mother and the others, my Aunt Blanche, Aunt Bessie and the boys, Erwin, Ray and Roy.

She said, "You know, that Roy was a real naughty little fellow at school. One day his teacher punished him by making him sit under her desk. He tied her shoestrings together and when she got up she couldn't walk. I don't think she ever punished him that way again. She probably made him stand in the corner. She didn't tell me."

"Grandma, when I was a little girl I loved to come to your house and stay all night. I remember that you always made biscuits, bacon and eggs for breakfast. I think you were so good to me because I was the oldest of ten children and we were so very poor."

"You didn't know you were poor. There seemed to be a lot of love in that family."

"I do remember once when we children were arguing about something and you said, 'Some day you will be far away from each other and wish you could be together.'

We stopped the argument then."

Grandma laughed. Strangely enough she was a beautiful young woman too. In heaven you can expect most anything.

I'd like to look up my Granddad Lewis also. He was always there for my brother, Harold, and me when we were kids. I don't remember that he went to church much, maybe more in his later years. I do remember that he became very ill before he died. Mother came home and told our family that her father had gone to be with the Lord. She said that he had lain in that bed in a near comatose state. Grandma and the sons and daughters were sitting around the bed just waiting.

Suddenly, Granddad sat up in bed. His eyes were bright and he obviously was seeing something none of the rest of them could see. He said "Glory, glory, glory!" I had never heard my grandfather use that word but it became a treasured word to me. When I chose to accept Christ in that old farmhouse closet I suddenly felt surrounded by light and found myself repeating the same refrain, "Glory, glory, glory!"

When my grandfather and I talk in heaven I shall ask him what he saw and did he step into Christ's presence at that time? I may ask him other things also, like "Granddad, I was so curious when I was a child about the missing third finger on your left hand. My mother told me once that you had an accident when working in a saw mill. Did you really feel a lot of pain? How did the whole thing happen? Were you a believer then? I'm so glad you and I can spend eternity together."

I may talk with my great grandmother Gaut. I didn't know her well when I was a child but we have a picture of her hanging on our wall. She looks so grim. Somehow, in the old days they didn't want people to smile when their picture was taken. The bits and pieces of memories I have of her are pleasant. One is that when she came to visit she always brought along her feather bed. Not yet school age, I begged to sleep with her and she welcomed me. I wet the bed but didn't get in trouble. Maybe I'll ask her why.

Once, when we lived in Missouri, Harold and I were being very naughty little kids. She told us to go out and get a "switch" off the shrub in front so she could punish us. We just laughed and I think she did, too. I also remember one time when she scolded my Mother for having on a dress with short sleeves. I thought it was silly. Such a pretty dress. But

Great Grandmother said, "Florence, you should be ashamed of yourself, showing off your bare, naked arms."

I know that at one time Great Grandmother smoked a corncob pipe. Now, that is not a wise thing to do. I don't think we ever saw her do it although Harold was hoping she would. And she had pierced ears. That must have happened when she was very young because she didn't wear earrings. She told me that only gypsies pierced their ears and they were very wicked. Now, I enjoy the lovely earrings I can get for my pierced ears. And I don't even feel wicked. I'll talk all those things over with Grandma Gaut when we discuss our lives on this earth.

Her husband, my great grandfather, fought in the Civil War. If he is in heaven I'd like to have a long discussion with him also. I think he was an aid to General Lee. I've heard General Lee was a Christian. I'd like to talk with him. Another great grandfather had been on the side of the north. I only saw pictures of both grandfathers. They had long beards in the pictures, a little bit stained with tobacco juice, I think.

The last few days Denny and Sharon have been visiting. Sharon's mother, Maxine, died a short time ago. Sharon is still grieving, of course. I'd like to have a conversation with Sharon's Mom, Maxine, and Sharon's Dad. Then we might all discuss with Jesus how grateful we were that He and the Father saw fit to give us such loving children. Denny said that they have pictures of Maxine as a girl when she was a carhop. Such a beautiful young woman she was. She is young and beautiful now, I'm sure. And, thankfully, no longer needs to be on dialysis.

Next, I'd like to look up my friend, Jeannette. She may be in choir practice because she had always told me that, because she couldn't carry a tune, she planned to be in God's heavenly choir. Then she would have a beautiful, perfect voice. Perhaps the Father granted her that desire.

Sure enough, there she is—singing her heart out. What a wonderful way to praise our Lord and Savior! I'd like to join that choir, too.

"Jeannette, have a cup of tea with me and let's have a long talk. I have been thinking what different childhoods we had while on earth. Was there ever a time, as a child, that you were aware of God's presence? Tell me some of the adventures you had as an "army brat". That's what you called yourself once."

"Well now, Betty, there was a time when a friend invited me to visit her Sunday School class and my mother let me go. They talked about Jesus and I was curious but didn't really know who they were talking about. Now, I've had the opportunity to see Him face to face and we have had some glorious visits."

"That is one of the joys of Heaven—being with Jesus and visiting for as long as we want. You are right, Jeannette, those visits are glorious."

"Yes, Betty, I am so glad God got my attention on earth and I had the opportunity to make Christ my Savior. I had never known that it was necessary to accept what Jesus did on the cross and commit my life to Him. There were a lot of wasted years before I discovered what it meant to be a Christian. Working with you in Bible Study Fellowship added to my understanding."

"And to mine, Jeannette. I had grown up thinking I had to be a "good girl" or I might lose my salvation. As we studied the Bible it became very clear that I couldn't be good enough to add anything to what Jesus had already done. He paid the price for my sins and nothing I did could add to that. Or subtract from it."

"And, Jeannette I want to let you know that after you had gone to be with the Lord I felt that I really hadn't done much to show you how I appreciated having you alongside of me in that ministry. You were such a loyal helper and I may not have said "thank you" when I should have. So I'm saying "thank you." I'm glad we are part of God's forever family and really are sisters. We have an eternity to fellowship. Praise the Lord!"

"Yes, praise the Lord!"

Because Bible Study Fellowship was such a vital part of my spiritual growth I have many memories of those who are now with our Lord. One of those is Barbara Ford.

"Oh, there you are, Barbara! You were so helpful as we ministered together in Bible study. Did I ever say 'Thank you' for all you did? Well, if I didn't, I'm saying it now, 'Thank You'! Also, didn't we have some great times comparing the antics of our respective grand children? I know you prayed consistently for yours, just I did for ours."

"Yes, Betty, and some of them will be with us. Some still must make that commitment. We can talk that over with Jesus. He loves them, too, you know."

"I know He does, Barbara. We can never love as Jesus loves. He gave His life while on earth as a man for all our loved ones. And I am glad we get to say 'Thank you' over and over to Him now."

This morning I am thinking of another Barbara who just this morning went to be with Jesus. Jennifer called from California to say that her mother-in-law, Barbara, had died this morning. Barbara and I often had discussed our children and grandchildren. While on earth we had a double interest in the affairs of our children. Barbara's daughter, Jennifer, married our son, Jerry, and our daughter, Jennifer, married Barbara's son, Mike. The grandchildren of those two unions blessed both Barbara and Rob and I. Perhaps Barbara and I can continue the family discussion in heaven.

I'd like to meet Martha Snell Nicholson because her little poem, Eternity, has been so helpful to me. She, of course, is a very sweet lady who loves our Lord deeply. I will walk up to her and say,

"Martha, I have been wishing to meet you since the brief time I lived on earth. I, too, wrote some poetry, free verse, not as fine as yours. Which reminds me, one of my friends who published a little book of poetry provided me with a chuckle. She wrote *Free Verse, Nothing's worse.* I may see her around here soon.

"As I said, I've wanted to meet and speak with you. Now that time doesn't matter we can get better acquainted. Once, I read your poem to a group of mentally handicapped adults. Those grown up 'children' understood perfectly what it meant to have their hand in God's hand. They also loved to pray and knew, without a doubt, that God heard and would answer them."

"Yes, Betty, I had struggled for a bit with my understanding of what God meant by eternity. Finally, that poem came to me."

"Perhaps the poem came right from the heart of God."

"That could be. I shall discuss it with Him."

"Martha, I want to give you a heavenly hug."

"That is permitted, my friend. We are all part of God's family and who wouldn't hug a brother or sister."

Just then, in my imagination, Jesus will walk up and add a hug for both of us.

"Jesus, I have been meaning to ask you. Why did you become a person, like us, and offer your life for mine? I know I didn't deserve it."

"My child, no one truly deserves it. Remember that you read in scripture that the Father so loved the world that He gave His only Son, that's Me, in order that you might live forever with us?"

"Yes, that was John 3:16. I think I learned it when I was young. The Bible was an important part of my life on earth. I believe I enjoyed most all those wonderful promises."

"Here is what I want you to know: Before the world began a plan was made for your life. You would receive eternal blessings. Psalm 21:6 tells you that. Have you spoken with my friend, David, who wrote that Psalm?"

"No, but I hope to do that soon."

"You must remember, Betty, that God's love and concern for you did not begin on the day you were born and end on the day you died physically. His concern, and mine reaches back to those days before you were born, and reaches along the unending path of eternity. There is so much planned for your eternal existence. It is more than you could imagine. By the way, isn't this place beautiful?"

"Oh, yes, Lord. This is what Eden must have been like. There is great joy. No more temptations, no more sin. When I read Rick Warren's book called *Heaven,* I remember that he said 'We were all made for a Person and a place. Jesus is the Person, heaven is the place.'

"Jesus, there is one more thing, did you hear me when I was awaiting the birth of each of our four children, and I dedicated that little being within me to God?"

"Yes, We heard and now they all belong to this wonderful Forever Family."

Printed in the United States
47007LVS00004B/1-225